TEXTS AND TRANSLATIONS 5

PSEUDEPIGRAPHA SERIES
4

THE TESTAMENT OF JOB

ACCORDING TO THE SV TEXT

Greek text and English translation
edited by Robert A. Kraft
with
Harold Attridge
Russell Spittler
Janet Timbie

SOCIETY OF BIBLICAL LITERATURE
&
SCHOLARS' PRESS
1974

Distributed by

SCHOLARS' PRESS

University of Montana

Missoula, Montana 59801

THE   TESTAMENT   OF   JOB

ACCORDING TO THE SV TEXT

Copyright © 1974

by

The Society of Biblical Literature

Library of Congress Catalog Card Number: 74-15201

ISBN: 0-88414-044-X

Printed in the United States of America

Printing Department

University of Montana

Missoula, Montana 59801

PREFACE TO THE SERIES

TEXTS AND TRANSLATIONS is a project of the Committee on Research and Publications of the Society of Biblical Literature and is under the general direction of George W. MacRae (Harvard Divinity School), Executive Secretary and Harry M. Orlinsky (Hebrew Union College-Jewish Institute of Religion, New York), Chairman of the Committee. The purpose of the project is to make available in convenient and inexpensive format ancient texts which are not easily accessible but are of importance to scholars and students of "biblical literature" as broadly defined by the Society. Reliable modern English translations will accompany the texts. Occasionally the various series will include documents not published elsewhere. It is not a primary aim of these publications to provide authoritative new critical texts, nor to furnish extensive annotations. The editions are regarded as provisional, and individual volumes may be replaced in the future as better textual evidence becomes available. The following subseries have been established thus far:

PSEUDEPIGRAPHA, edited by Robert A. Kraft (University of Pennsylvania)

GRECO-ROMAN RELIGION, edited by Hans Dieter Betz (School of Theology at Claremont)

EARLY CHRISTIAN LITERATURE, edited by Birger A. Pearson (Univeristy of California at Santa Barbara)

For the PSEUDEPIGRAPHA SERIES the choice of texts is governed in part by the research interests of the SBL Pseudepigrapha Group, of which George W.E. Nickelsburg, Jr. (University of Iowa) is currently Chairman and James H. Charlesworth (Duke University) Secretary. This series will focus on Jewish materials from the Hellenistic era and will regularly include volumes that incorporate the fragmentary evidence of works attributed to biblical personalities, culled from a wide range of Jewish and Christian sources. The volumes are selected, prepared, and edited in consultation with the following editorial subcommittee of the Pseudepigrapha Group:

Sebastian P. Brock (Cambridge University, England)

George W. MacRae (Harvard Divinity School)

George W.E. Nickelsburg, Jr. (University of Iowa)

Michael E. Stone (Hebrew University, Israel)

John Strugnell (Harvard Divinity School)

Robert A. Kraft, Editor

TABLE OF CONTENTS

INTRODUCTION	1
WITNESSES TO THE TEXT	2
THE TEXT: GENERAL	3
GENEALOGICAL RELATIONSHIPS WITHIN PSV	6
SELECTED ORTHOGRAPHIC AND SYNTACTIC PECULIARITIES IN THE SV TEXT	8
THE GREEK TEXT OF THE PRESENT EDITION	9
THE TRANSLATION, APPARATUS, VERSIFICATION	10
ANNOTATED CHRONOLOGICAL BIBLIOGRAPHY (by R.Spittler)	11
TEXT, TRANSLATION, APPARATUS	15

INTRODUCTION AND ACKNOWLEDGMENTS

In October 1973, the Steering Committee of the SBL Pseudepigrapha Group decided to devote its 1974 symposium to a discussion of the TESTAMENT OF JOB. It was agreed that a readily available translation of T. Job would be desirable for the 1974 discussions, and I was asked to coordinate efforts towards the appearance of the desired material in the TEXTS AND TRANSLATIONS SERIES.

The original suggestion was relatively simple: Russell Spittler had recently included an English translation of T. Job in his Harvard doctoral thesis (1971), based mainly on Sebastian Brock's 1967 edition of the Greek text, which is still available. Thus the possibility of reproducing the actual photographs of the oldest Greek witness (P) alongside a revision of Spittler's translation was suggested for exploration. Subsequent investigation led to significant modifications of this plan when it was recognized that an eclectic critical edition of T. Job was still needed (Brock reedited the text of P, with a full apparatus of S and V variations), and that the text represented most clearly in MS S had received little attention in the past. Thus it was decided to do for S what Brock had done for P, namely, to "correct" the most obvious errors and produce an idealized hypothetical archetype preserving the characteristics of the S stream.

A number of people collaborated towards this end. Spittler allowed his material to be used in whatever way seemed most helpful and prepared the annotated bibliography. Harold Attridge painstakingly worked through the text and translation and supplied numerous helpful suggestions at various points. Brock sent us his photographs of S for first-hand examination as well as offering advice and encouragement. Others also contributed in various ways (John Collins, Howard Kee, and Berndt Schaller). But the brunt of the continuing work of preparation was borne by members of my Spring 1974 graduate seminar (Margaret McKenna, Ruth Sandberg, Ross Kraemer, and especially Janet Timbie), who worked through many of the problems of the text of T. Job with me, and cooperated in compiling a card file of the Greek vocabulary (including variants). Janet Timbie also prepared the penultimate draft of the translation (adjusting the work of Spittler and Attridge to the "S text") and typed the Greek text for reproduction. Linda Wiedmann of the General Honors and Religious Thought Offices patiently and skillfully transformed the heavily annotated hand-written materials into the present typed form of the translation and apparatus. Finally, the advice and encouragement of the SBL Pseudepigrapha Group steering committee and of the Pseudepigrapha Series editorial board have also been invaluable.

University of Pennsylvania
June, 1974

Robert A. Kraft, editor

WITNESSES TO THE TEXT

Known witnesses to the text of T.Job include four Greek manuscripts, a fragmentary 5th century Coptic MS, and a Slavonic (old church Slavic) version resonstructed from three MSS.

- P = Paris Bibliothéque Nationale grec 2658. Small quarto vellum codex ("petit" format = less than 27cm) with 23 lines/page, written in a "fine hand" from the 11th century (or 10th[1]). Contains: Meanings of Hebrew Names in Scripture (fol 1a); Testaments of the 12 Patriarchs (1b-72a = Charles' MS_f_); T.Job (72a-97a); and Anastasius of Sinai, Questions and Answers (98a-224 with ending missing; seems to be written in an earlier hand [James]). Editions by James and Brock.
- (P_2) = Paris Bibliothéque Nationale grec 938. Small quarto paper codex in "petit" format, from the 16th century. Contains 12 writings, of which the Meanings of Hebrew Names, Testaments of the 12 Patriarchs, and T.Job (fol 172b-192b) are at the end after nine patristic texts. According to James (lxxiii) and Brock (5), P_2 is a copy made from P, and thus has no independent value for text critical purposes (details in Brock 10).
- V = Rome, Vatican gr. 1238. Vellum codex (palimpsest with 12th century underwriting in parts) supplemented with paper in early portions; 31 x 20 cm, 33-39 lines/page, now bound in 3 volumes; dated 1195 according to Rahlfs[2] or 13th century (Charles, Brock). Contains: Octateuch + Samuel-Kings + 2 Chronicles 1.1-13.15 (designated as # 246 in Rahlfs/Göttingen notation), T.Job (fol 340a-349b), and Testaments of the 12 Patriarchs (fol 350-380 = Charles' _d_). Edition by Mai, with corrections in James, Spitta and Brock.
- S = Messina (Sicily), San Salvatore 29. Vellum codex, 42.8 x 33.4 cm with 2 cols/page and about 43 lines/col (30± letters/line) dated 1307 (Rahlfs, Brock) or 1308 (Analecta Bolland. 23 [1904], 33). Latter part of Menologion of Daniel the monk (first part in cod.30) (some leaves are palimpsests reusing 6-7th or 8-9th century Psalm Commentary--see Rahlfs 136), with T.Job (fol 35b-41b) as "item 8" for May 6 (the dates and item numbers are not consistent), followed by Ps-Chrysostom, Homily 2 on Job (see PG 56.567-570) as "item 9." Collated by Mancini.
- cop = Papyrus Cologne 3221. Fragments of a Sahidic codex (with Bohairic influences) dated to 5th century and including T.Abraham as well as T.Job. Chs 26-53 of T.Job are better preserved than chs 1-25. Manfred Weber of the Institut für Altertumskunde at the University of Cologne is in charge of editing the text. Preliminary details in Philonenko 61-63.
- slav = the material published by Polivka, based on one complete Slavic MS (once owned by P.J.Šafaric) with readings from two others (Belgrade National Library 149, Moscow Rumjancov Museum 1472) also noted. Possibly dates from 10th century (Spittler "?").

---

[1] R.H.Charles, _The Greek Versions of the Testaments of the Twelve Patriarchs_ (Oxford Univ., 1908) xi (confused with P_2).
[2] A.Rahlfs, _Verzeichnis der griechischen Handschriften des Alten Testaments_ (Berlin, 1914) 261.

THE TEXT OF THE TESTAMENT OF JOB: GENERAL

An up to date assessment of the relationships between the preserved witnesses to the text of T.Job must now await the full publication of the fragments of the earliest known witness--the Coptic version. Meanwhile, Brock's apparatus provides us with a convenient collection of all significant variations in the Greek texts and a sampling of Slavonic readings. Even apart from the problems presented by the Coptic and Slavonic witnesses, however, and despite the careful text critical observations made by such editors as James, Mancini, and Brock, much room remains for development of a careful, methodologically self-conscious approach to the text of T.Job.

This is not the place for a detailed treatment of the issues. Nevertheless, a few observations may be useful, while the data involved in preparing this edition are still fresh in the editor's mind.

It is quite clear that no direct and immediate relationship exists between P, S or V. MSS P and V stand farthest apart from each other, while S stands somewhere between them. In statistical terms, which can be very misleading if given undue or misplaced emphasis, the situation is roughly as follows (for the most part, the figures are approximate and hastily compiled):

```
SP agree against V more than 300 times   (% of quantitative undetermined)
SV agree against P about      206 times  (55% are quantitative in nature)
PV agree against S about       87 times  (72% are quantitative in nature)
[statistics on passages in which P versus S versus V have not been compiled]
```

V   The unsupported (by SP) readings of V range from transpositions and minor quantitative ("plusses", "minuses") and qualitative (alternative words and passages) variation to the inclusion/exclusion of entire sentences or radically different wording. For the most part, the V text reads very smoothly and often "clarifies" ambiguities in the parallel SP material or streamlines difficult and/or repetitive contexts. I have little doubt that V is a developed representative of self-conscious recensional activity applied to the text of T.Job, possibly over a rather long period of time (that is, V probably is not a single maverick MS, but is part of a branch of textual development characterized by the same general phenomena). The origins and stages of this activity are lost to our present view, although I suspect that a closer comparison of V and slav might be revealing--note e.g. the significant agreements between Vslav on chronology (see 21.1, 22.1, 26.1b), or their agreement in the opening verses of the book. The numerous agreements of SV against P, however, suggest that at one point in the development of the V stream, the text being "revised" looked more like what we now have in S than what is preserved for us in P (see further below).

P   The unsupported (by SV) readings of P usually are not so far-ranging in their "deviation" as those of V. The text of P is also usually quite intelligible, however, and may itself show signs of restrained, but nontheless self-conscious recensional work at some point or points in its development--I say "may" because it is often extremely difficult to determine whether the problematic readings in P should be dismissed as "secondary" or embraced as "ancient" (if not "original"). I think the question of whether P represents self-conscious recensional activity (rather than merely haphazard variation) is important enough to permit a few examples--it is a question that has not received much attention from earlier editors:

(1) P contains a greater number of compound verbal stems than does the SV material in the same passages. In 31 instances in which P differs from S on this matter, the following situation obtains:

SV simple, P compound	14		P simple, SVcompound	4	
S simple, P compound (no V)	3		P simple, S compound (no V)	3	
S simple, PV compound	4		PV simple, S compound	3	
	21			10	

What the significance (if any) of such a phenomenon may be for the history of the text of T.Job remains to be determined. It is sometimes stated that compound forms tend to become more frequent in second century (CE) Christian writings than in earlier ones. The wider question of preferences and usages in Jewish and Christian Greek texts from hellenistic times on into the 11th to 12th centuries is of crucial importance here.

(2) P contains the divine epithet "Father" in several passages where SV have "God" or "Lord." Nevertheless, all three Greek texts have "Father" in 33.9b (see also 50.3 "paternal (patrikēs) splendor" PV/om context S), and perhaps "Father" was also the reading of the PSV archetype at 33.3b, where V has the abbreviation for "savior" (srs) which closely resembles that for "Father" (prs) in P, while S has "God" (ths). But note also the following:

40.3 "to the Father" (pros ton patera) P: "first to the Lord and to God" (prōton tō kō [=kyriō] kai thō [=theō]) S(slav om first): "to God first" (tō thō prōton) V. The confusion of proston and prōton is understandable, and the pros construction seems more awkward (as opposed to a simple dative) and perhaps thus "secondary." Does that also make the reading "Father" more suspect?
47.11 "Father" P: "Lord" SVslav.
52.6 "Father" P: "God" SVslav.

Whether the change went from "God/Lord" to "Father" or vice-versa in these passages is open to debate. Especially in chs. 39-53, Job is called "father" on several occasions (1.3a, 46.3a, 46.3b, 47.1b, 47.3a, 48.1, 52.4 [?], 53.1b). Perhaps the SV(slav) stream attempted to avoid confusion by emending the texts that refer to deity. Or perhaps somewhere in the P stream the change was made because of habit or preference in referring to God as "Father" (note that even P elsewhere frequently uses "Lord" [37 times] and "God" [16 times]). I must confess that although I think "Father" may have been in the archetype of PSV in 33.3b as well as in 33.9b, I suspect that it is secondary in the other passages (see also Brock 8). Whether it was "original" in 33.3b and 9b is another question--the PSV archetype could already be "secondary" at that point (and a witness to an earlier step towards the development that continued in the P stream).

(3) P contains the diminutive teknia (see also Testaments of the 12 Patriarchs and Gospel of John) where S(V) have tekna in 5.1a, 5.2, 6.1a, 45.5 and 47.11. Elsewhere in T.Job all three Greek MSS have tekna (including six other occurrences in direct address). Probably the P reading is "secondary" here, unless the PSV archetype was inconsistent or had teknia throughout, and SV changed to tekna throughout (with P producing or retaining the inconsistency that now exists).

(4) In the lament in ch. 32, the repeated refrain probably originally read "Where NOW (nun)..."(if we can assume consistency in the original form!). But in 32.2b, 3b, 4b, 10c, 11c we find that P has "Where THEN (oun)..." P seems secondary, perhaps entirely accidentally, but similar arguments as outlined in (3) above regarding the SPV archetype and its consistency or lack of such also apply here.

S   The significant unsupported (by PV) readings of S are predominantly quantitative in nature, usually "minuses"/omissions, but also a significant number of "plusses" (almost 40% of the quantitative variants). Frequently the "minus" texts seem to be the result of careless copying--haplography, homoioteleuton, etc. The "plusses" are usually articles, conjunctions, pronouns, etc. The only "plusses" of more than a word or two come in 4.1b, 32.1b, and in the dittography at 40.11 (see also the relatively significant plusses in 16.3, 21.2a, 23.2, 32.12c [note at 2b], 34.5, 40.4a, 47.1b). The minuses are also usually very minor, except for a few in chs. 40-53 (see 34.1b, 40.10-11, 44.5b-6, 47.7, 49.2, 50.3, 51.3). The qualitative variants (alternative readings) usually are also very minor, and frequently involve only a few letters. Indeed, because the orthography of S is so "wild" (see Brock 8f), it is not easy to determine when a variant should be ascribed to orthographic confusion and when it should really be counted (e.g. "me" [me] might be written in S as mē [lit. "not"] and perhaps even as moi [lit. "to me"], etc.) But a few relatively noteworthy variants do occur, as in the title, 4.1b, 15.10b, 33.4b.

In short, S seems to be very "conservative," if carelessly copied, by comparison to both V and P. The only "recensional" tendency I have observed in S is in a few passages where phrases paralleled in the Greek of the biblical book of Job appear, and S tends to support the BS text of Job while PV support the A text (e.g. 15.10b = Job 1.5 [see also Job 14.8, 22.5]; 26.1c and 3 = Job 2.9e; see also 24.1b = Job 2.9a). This bears further investigation when an adequate critical apparatus for the Greek of Job becomes available.

GENEALOGICAL RELATIONSHIPS WITHIN PSV

On the basis of the general statistics provided above, one might be tempted to argue that SP have a closer genealogical relationship than do SV or PV (indeed there can be little question of PV being related genealogically). But such relationships must, for the most part, be determined by isolating agreements between witnesses in erroneous (or "secondary") readings in which an earlier text form (archetype) has been modified; agreement in correct readings tells nothing about genealogical relationships. Furthermore, agreement in omission is theoretically less significant than are secondary additions or alternative readings, since independent, coincidental agreement in omission is theoretically more likely than independent agreement in addition or variation. Thus, to establish a characteristically SP branch of the textual tradition one must be able to show passages in which the reading of V is more ancient (or "original") than that of SP. In fact, this situation almost never seems to arise. Possible exceptions of note include the tense of the verb "to be" in 2.1, the inclusion of "her" by V (om SP) in 25.4b, 7b, the spelling Eliphaz (-phas SP) in 29.3a, and the reading Eliphaz (Elious PS) in 33.1. But such minor readings can be explained satisfactorily by other means such as "correction" by V to agree with the context or with parallel passages in T.Job. Apparently SP have such a wide range of agreement not because of some unique genealogical relationship over against V, but because they preserve more faithfully the textual base common to PSV, from which all three texts have developed--and the V text has modified that base a large percent of the time.

Is there stronger evidence for positing a unique genealogical relationship between S and V where they agree against P? Again, the required evidence must be readings common to SV which are secondary to those in P. There are a number of major quantitative minuses in SV that might suggest that an archetype of SV was defective at these points--e.g. 9.8-9, 13.2, 28.3, 32.7 and 13, 36.6b, 37.11-38.1, 41.4, 43.9a. The possibility of independent omission by S and V or of additions in the P stream (see also 14.5 P, possibly originally a marginal gloss) is present--it is even strong in a few instances--but the cumulative impression suggests a special relationship of SV, in comparison to P. (The basic similarity between SVslav in the subscript, which P lacks, also points in this direction.)

Convincing supporting evidence from qualitative variations in which SV agree against P is not easy to isolate. Usually both SV and P have "reasonable" readings where they disagree, and it is difficult to determine which may be secondary (as we noted in some examples given above, discussing P). Perhaps such readings as 37.10 deixon P / didaxon SV, or 48.3 dialektō P / phonē SV show SV to be secondary, since in both, P uses a word attested elsewhere in similar contexts in T.Job while the SV text does not. But intelligent counter-arguments can be offered as well (e.g. harmonization by P). The important, if tiny, variation in 40.8 is again equally frustrating--did Sitidos die "cheerfully" (euth-) as in P, or (the more difficult reading) "with resignation"/"untroubled" (if that is the meaning: ath-) as in SV? Either makes sense in the context. Such examples could be multiplied, including orthographic differences (see p.8).

The most interesting example I have encountered on this question of the genealogical significance of SV agreements is in 32.9b-c. Judging from the pattern exhibited throughout the surrounding "lament," the refrain (32.9b) should also appear at the end of 32.9. But in SV it disruptively divides 9a from 9c, while it is entirely absent from P. It is probable that the corruption (if we can assume the expected consistency in the original of T.Job) is as old as the common text behind PSV: either the lines were already transposed in that archetype (with the SV text faithfully preserving the transposition) and the P stream subsequently dropped the refrain by accident or design, or the refrain was already omitted in the archetype (accurately reflected now in P) and was reintroduced (via the margin?) but misplaced in the SV stream. Possible, but perhaps less probable, is that the PSV archetype had the expected sequence and content, but that the SV archetype transposed it and the P archetype independently omitted the refrain (by accident).

The question, then, is whether the evidence is adequate to establish that SV derive from a single textual development that deviated from the PSV archetype in a manner parallel to the development of the P stream--that is, are we dealing basically with only two offshoots (P and SV) of the PSV common base? This seems to be somewhat more probable than the alternative possibility that each preserved Greek text attests a separate and independent development from a common PSV archetype--a three branched genealogy. Hopefully the Coptic material will shed further light on this problem--informal preliminary reports indicate that it supports the two branch stemma. If a three branched stemma were accepted, the (independent) agreements of any two MSS against the other ("majority" principle) become more valuable as indicators of the text of the PSV archetype than would otherwise be true. In a two branched stemma, the SV agreements help establish the SV archetype, which then must be evaluated against P to determine the PSV base text. (The relation of the PSV archetype to the "original" of T.Job must then be considered.) If we assume the basic validity of a two branch stemma, the present edition constitutes an attempt only to recover the SV branch. If a three branch stemma were accepted, the present edition would come much closer to being an eclectic reconstruction of the PSV archetype!

To illustrate further the complexities involved in attempting to recreate an SV archetype and ultimately move behind it towards the "original" text of T.Job, the following examples of particularly interesting and/or difficult passages/phenomena are offered. Others could easily be added to the list.

SELECTED ORTHOGRAPHIC AND SYNTACTIC PECULIARITIES IN THE SV TEXT

Spelling and unusual words (on orthography of S, see Brock 8-9):

7.1 ἀσσάλιον PSV (see note in apparatus at 7.1)

ἀγμήν =SV in 27.7 and 34.4 (ἀκμήν P) and =S in 34.6 (αὐτός V; ἀκμήν P). In all these passages the word seems to refer to "the moment of truth" in a contest, and may be a special term from the idiom of competitive events. Because the spelling ἀγμήν does not appear in standard lexicons, the P form has been printed below, but with much hesitation on the part of the editor. In 7.9, ἀκμήν appears in SP (om V) in a different sort of context.

The forms of ἀφορίζειν in 9.2b (ἀφόριζα SV: ἀφώρισα P), 9.5b (ἠφόριζα SV: ἀφόρησα P), and 10.5c (ἠφόριζα S: ἀφόριζον V: ἀφορίζειν P) present a problem; the same verb appears also in 38.5 in a standard form. Presumably the verbal forms in 9.2b and 5b should be identical--either aorist (so Brock emends 5b; see also the pattern in 9.4b, 10.5b, 10.6) or possibly imperfect (ἀφώριζον cj Attridge as alternative to aorist). Again in 10.5c, aorist or imperfect would fit well. The near consistency of SV in these passages would seem to require some explanation, as well as the variety in P. Probably the PSV archetype was corrupt/inconsistent in at least some of these passages. (See further Brock 14.)

The use of -σσ-/-ττ- in the words περισσός and κρείσσων is not consistent in the MSS. περισσός appears only in 15.6 P (-ττ- SV); otherwise the -ττ- spelling occurs in 15.5 SV (om context P), 24.5a SV (om P), 47.1b SP (om V), and only in V in 11.3b. κρείσσων appears only in 27.10 SV (-ττ- P); otherwise the -ττ- form is used--18.6c, 18.7, 46.5, 47.1b, in all MSS.

κράβαττος is the spelling used by SV, while P has κράββατος in every occurrence of the word (18.4, 25.7a, 32.5a).

In 30.1b and 3b, we find the spelling κατερρημένους (SV: κατερριγμένων P) and ἐρρημένων (SP: δεδομένων V) instead of the more normal -ρρυη-.

In 15.9, SV have βδέλλυγμα (βδέλυγμα P), and in 24.10 ἐγκακήσασα (ἐκκ-P).

Syntactical anomalies and/or corruptions of special note:

13.1-3 The subject of 13.2 in SV is not clear (for P it is the cattle). Nor is it clear how V construes 13.1: James thinks V took διεφώνουν to mean "to call to" (the milkers call to travelers to share the abundance?), while for P(S) it means "grow weary, faint, fail" (p. lxxxviii).

15.3a τὰ δὲ ἐπικείμενα SP (om context V): αἱ δὲ ἐπικείμεναι cj Attridge.

18.3-4 Apparently Sslav have something about seeing "those who make lamps" (ποιοῦντας : -ες cj Kraft), and in SV, "men" at the end of 18.4 is in the nominative (S supplies a verb), but accusative in P.

24.6-7 The sequence of verbs (mostly infinitives) in SP is awkward (V has a smoother reading text:
P = τολμῆσαι...ἐξελθεῖν...κατανύγομαι...(om context)...δεῖξαι...ἀκοῦσαι
S = τολμῆσαι...ἐξελθεῖν...κατανυγήσαφα...εἶπε⟨ῖ⟩ν   ...δεῖξαι...ἀκοῦσαι
V = ἐτόλμησα...   ἐλθεῖν...(om context)...εἴποντος   ...ἔδειξα...ἤκουσα

Perhaps in 26.3 ἵνα (so P: om SV) should be inserted before ἀπαλλοτριωθῶμεν (cj Attridge). See also the apparatus at 26.3.

37.5 See the discussion in the apparatus.

37.11-38.1 (and surrounding context) See the apparatus.

46.9 Perhaps emend the genitive (μίας = S^cV) ἑκάστης (om P) to dative (cj Attridge) and the subsequent command λάβετε αὐτάς to λάβετε ⟨αὐτὰς καὶ περιζώσατε⟩ αὐτάς (see V, and 47.5, 47.7, 48.1, 49.1, 50.1).

48.4 See suggestions in the apparatus.

53.1-4 The introductory material in 53.1 contains no main verb.

THE GREEK TEXT OF THE PRESENT EDITION: PRINCIPLES EMPLOYED

The goal of this edition is to recreate as closely as possible the basic text ("archetype") that presumably lies behind the present forms of S and V. The following guidelines have been followed, although occasional inconsistency may sometimes occur in the editor's judgments (orthographic and related problems in S have been tacitly adjusted to current convention):

(1) Where SV agree against P and present an intelligible text, the Greek of SV is printed--the main exceptions to this rule are when P seems to supply material not present in SV but necessary for the sense of the passage (e.g. 9.8-9, 25.8a, 28.3, 32.10a, 38.1, 43.9a, 48.1).

(2) Where PV agree against S, it is usually assumed that the S reading is secondary, especially when S has a shorter text--exceptions to this rule include several passages in which it seems possible that a longer ("plus") text in S may have been abbreviated independently by P and V (3.1a, 4.1b, 8.2, 11.3a, 18.3, 18.7, 27.2c, 28.5, 30.1b, 32.1b, 37.12b, 40.4a, 51.3) or a shorter ("minus") text in S has been supplemented independently (7.8a, 32.9c, 40.8, 52.1a, 53.1a); non-quantitative exceptions include the title, 4.1b, and 41.7, where coincidental agreement between P and V seems quite possible.

(3) Where V goes its own way (as is frequent) and S differs from P, the reading of S usually is adopted if it is sufficiently intelligible--exceptions include 1.3b, 2.2, 18.5, 31.1b, 33.3b, 39.1 (twice), 40.7, 43.4a, 44.1, 47.12, 53.2.

(4) Occasionally conjectural emendation seems necessary in attempting to recover the SV textual base (e.g. 9.4b, 24.6-7, 26.2-3, 27.2c, 40.10-11, 53.1b); at times the editor's enthusiasm may have led him to look beyond the presumed SV base towards at least the PSV archetype if not the "original" form of T.Job (e.g. 7.4a, 25.5b, 37.5b, 37.12-38.1, 40.14, 43.9a, 48.1). At other times, however, where the SV reading seems clear, such conjectures are suggested in the notes rather than included in the printed text. It should be noted that the SV base text itself probably was corrupt at several points; in many instances it would be difficult to recreate such corruptions with precision, even if that were desirable. (Nor should one lose sight of the possibility that there may have been "corruptions" even in the earliest text of a work like T.Job, if the author/editor employed earlier traditions/sources in his work.) Thus in some ways the text offered below is a step towards an eclectic text of T.Job, although it is not intended to be such an eclectic text in itself.

THE TRANSLATION, APPARATUS, VERSIFICATION

Spittler's translation aimed at being "literal without severely compromising English idiom." The following revision and adaptation of his work attempts to retain the concern for both faithfulness to the Greek, and English readability. Occasionally we found no suitable way to resolve awkwardness without resorting to free paraphrase, but felt it would be more useful to retain the awkwardness. We beg the reader's indulgence at those points.

The "established" verse divisions inherited by Brock-Spittler (etc.) proved to be so unsuited to our task that we finally abandoned hope of using them throughout. They are noted in parentheses where they differ from the new versification introduced here. Versification is, of course, affected not only by the actual words in the text being studied, but also by how one interprets the sense units he sees in that text. Occasionally we have tried to make allowances for textual differences between P and our text (see especially 32.7 and 13!). The chapter divisions established by James and used by subsequent editors, however, have been retained even when they occasionally seem rather incongruous (see e.g. 1.6, 28.8, 38.9). For a "concordance to the chapter numeration in James and Kohler" (which differs radically), see Brock 17.

The apparatus does not aim at noting <u>all</u> variants (Brock must be consulted for this), but does attempt to present virtually all of the translationally significant variants, as well as some translation alternatives and an occasional critical observation concerning a particular text or word. It is hoped that the abbreviations and symbols used in the apparatus will be self-explanatory. The main sigla appear below:

```
< >         encloses material absent from S but supplied from another source
x - y       all phraseology from x through y is under consideration
x...y       only the x and y portions of the phraseology are under consideration
+           extra material, quantitative "plus" ("addition")
S(P)        P supports, but is not exactly identical with the S reading
Job 1.10 ABS  the form of the biblical text supported by codex
              A(lexandrinus), B(=Vaticanus), S(=Sinaiticus), etc.
```

cj	conjectured by	MS(S)	manuscript(s)
cop	Coptic version	om	material lacking, quantitative "minus" ("omitted")
fem.	feminine		
gk	Greek text	pl.	plural
infin.	infinitival form	pr	material precedes
lit.	literal meaning	sing.	singular
masc.	masculine	slav	Slavonic version

ANNOTATED CHRONOLOGICAL BIBLIOGRAPHY

compiled by Russell Spittler

This bibliography is offered as an attempt to survey efficiently the history of research on T.Job. Some entries (especially certain encyclopedia articles) are included for general interest, even though they offer nothing original or new for the advancement of scholarship on T.Job. No attempt has been made to be comprehensive on such items.

1833   Mai, A. SCRIPTORUM VETERUM NOVA COLLECTIO E VATICANIS CODICIBUS (Vatican, Rome) 7, 180-91. Editio princeps, using the V text. The sole note to the text concludes from the term anestēse in the subscript that the work is Christian.

1858   Migne, J.P. DICTIONNAIRE DES APOCRYPHES = Troisième et dernière encyclopédie théologique 23-24 (Migne, Paris) 2, 401-20. First modern language translation (French), based on Mai's text (=V).

1878   Novaković, S. "Apokrifua priča o Jovu," STARINE 10, 157-70. An edition of one of the Old Church Slavic MSS (=N); since half of the MS was missing, the editor put that portion of T.Job into Serbocroation from Migne's French translation.

1891   Polivka, G. "Apokrifna priča o Jovu," STARINE 24, 135-55. Critical edition of the three Old Church Slavic MSS.

1897   James, M.R. APOCRYPHA ANECDOTA 2 = Texts and Studies 5.1 (Cambridge Univ. Press). Introduction to T.Job on pp. lxxii-cii; Greek text of P (with some V variants noted from Mai) on pp. 104-37. Standard text, with chapter divisions, used until Brock. Helpful introductory material; biblical parallels cited. "If we think of [the author] as a Jew by birth, a Christian by faith, and as living in Egypt in the second or third century, we shall not, I believe, be far wrong.... He was putting into Greek a Hebrew Midrash on Job...His work is not a literal translation of a Hebrew original: it is rather a paraphrase thereof in Greek...Our author felt at liberty to make some additions to his original--...the longer speeches, the hymns [in chs 25, 32, 33, 43], the similes [in chs 4, 18, 27], and the whole of chs 46-52, will have been inserted by the man who put the story into Greek" (xciv-xcvi). A similar technique of Christian Greek paraphrasing to that used in History of Asenath.

1897   Bonwetsch, N. Review of James' ed. in THEOLOGISCHE LITERATURZEITUNG 19, 510. Mentions existence of the Slavonic material.

1898   Kohler, K. "The Testament of Job: an Essene Midrash on the Book of Job reedited and translated with introductory and exegetical notes," in SEMITIC STUDIES IN MEMORY OF A. KOHUT, ed. G.A.Kohut (Calvary & Co., Berlin), 264-338 (with addenda and corregenda on 611f). Mai's Greek text (=V) with English translation (sometimes flawed) and chapter/verse divisions differing from those of James. Introduction focuses on Semitic (especially Rabbinic and Muslim) folklore about Job. Sees T.Job as originating from Therapeutae "in the outskirts of Palestine in the land of Hauran, where the Nabatheans lived, and the Essene brotherhoods spread it all over the Arabian lands" (295).

1898   Battifol, P. Review of James' ed. in REVUE BIBLIQUE 7, 302-304.

1901   Conybeare, F. "The Testament of Job and the Testaments of the XII Patriarchs," JEWISH QUARTERLY REVIEW 13, 111-13 (127). Transcribes the V text of 1.1-2 and 47.10-end, without significant comment.

1901   Kohler, K. (and Toy, C.H.). "Job, Testament of," in JEWISH ENCYCLOPEDIA 7, 200-202. Brief survey of scholarship followed by lengthy summary of contents. "The work is one of the most remarkable productions of the pre-Christian era, explicable only when viewed in the light of ancient Hasidean practice."

1905   Beer, G. "Pseudepigraphen des AT" (no. 32_3 = T.Job), in REALENCYKLOPÄDIE FÜR PROTESTANTISCHE THEOLOGIE UND KIRCHE[3] 16, 256 (= NEW SCHAFF-HERZOG ENCYCLOPAEDIA OF RELIGIOUS KNOWLEDGE 9, 340). Bare mention of T.Job.

1907   Spitta, F. "Das Testament Hiobs und das Neue Testament," ZUR GESCHICHTE UND LITERATUR DES URCHRISTENTUMS 3.2 (Vandehoeck and Ruprecht, Göttingen), 139-206. T.Job is a pre-Christian but not Essene product of Jewish popular piety and furnished NT writers with a model for Jesus as sufferer. Includes some notes provided by James correcting Mai's text of V.

1909   Schürer, E. GESCHICHTE DES JÜDISCHEN VOLKES IM ZEITALTER JESUS CHRISTI[4] (Hinrichs, Leipzig) 3, 406f. (earlier editions contain no mention of T.Job.). Follows James, despite Spitta's arguments, in seeing T.Job as a Christian work.

1910/25 Ginzberg, L. LEGENDS OF THE JEWS (Jewish Publ. Soc., Philadelphia) 2, 225-42, and notes in 5, 381-90. Synthetic overview of Jewish materials on Job, including T.Job.

1911   Charles, R.H. "Apocalyptic Literature," in ENCYCLOPEDIA BRITTANICA[11] 2, 169-75. Refers favorably to Kohler's theory of Essenic origin for T.Job. (Charles did not include T.Job in his 1913 collection of APOCRYPHA AND PSEUDEPIGRAPHA OF THE OT.)

1911   Mancini, A. "Per la Critica del 'Testamentum Job,'" RENDICONTI DELLA REALE ACCADEMIA DEI LINCEI 20, 479-502. Collation of S with P (James) and V (Mai), with some philological and text critical observations.

1913   James, M.R. OLD TESTAMENT LEGENDS, BEING STORIES OUT OF SOME OF THE LESS-KNOWN APOCRYPHAL BOOKS OF THE OT (Longmans-Green, London). A simplified and selective paraphrase of T.Job appears in this story-book dedicated to James' grandchildren.

1915   Thomson, J.E.H. "Apocalyptic Literature IV: Testaments, (4) Testament of Job," INTERNATIONAL STANDARD BIBLE ENCYCLOPEDIA 1, 177-78. Palestinian (?) Jewish work translated into Greek by a Christian, with some additions.

1920   James, M.R. THE LOST APOCRYPHA OF THE OT--THEIR TITLES AND FRAGMENTS = Translations of Early Documents Series 1.14 (SPCK, London), 93. Reports the suggestion of H.Bate that T.Job 20.9 is alluded to by Tertullian in de bono patientiae 13.

1926   Bousset, W. and Gressman, H. DIE RELIGION DES JUDENTUMS IM SPÄTHELLENISTISCHEN ZEITALTER[3] = Handbuch zum NT 21 (Mohr, Tübingen), 45. T.Job contains Jewish legends with traces of Christian editing.

1928   Frey, J.B. "Apocryphes de l'Ancien Testament" (No.16 = Quelques apocryphes plus tardifs ou fragmentaires: 2 Le Testament de Job), in DICTIONNAIRE DE LA BIBLE, Supplement 1, 455. General summary of past research.

1928   Fuchs, J. "Hiobs Testament," in JUDISCHES LEXIKON 2, 1613.

1928   Riessler, P. ALTJÜDISCHES SCHRIFTTUM AUSSERHALB DER BIBEL (Filser, Augsburg), 1104-34 (German translation with new versification later followed by Brock), and 1333-34 (introduction and notes). Sees T.Job as an Essenic Hebrew midrash on Job composed in the first century BCE and later rendered paraphrastically into Greek.

1931   Bernfeld, I. "Hiobs Testament," in ENCYCLOPEDIA JUDAICA 8, 74f. A propaganda document emphasizing conversion of pagan to Judaism; potentially useful for Christians as well as Jews.

1936/37 Kahana, A. HA-SEFARIM HA-HIṢONIM (Tel Aviv) 1, 515-38. Modern Hebrew translation using Riessler's chapter/verse divisions (1956^2)

1945   Torrey, C.C. THE APOCRYPHAL LITERATURE: A BRIEF INTRODUCTION (Yale Univ. Press), 140-45. Posits 1st cent. BCE Aramaic original.

1946   Gerleman, G. STUDIES IN THE SEPTUAGINT BOOK OF JOB = Lund Universitets Årsskrift 43.2, 60-63. The Appendix to LXX Job may derive from possible Hebrew original of T.Job.

1949   Pfeiffer, R.H. HISTORY OF NT TIMES... (Harper), 70-72 [see also his articles in INTERPRETERS BIBLE (1952) 1, 425, and in THE TWENTIETH CENTURY ENCYCLOPEDIA OF RELIGIOUS KNOWLEDGE 2 (1955), 925]. "A pre-Christian legendary biography [midrash] written in Aramaic [in Palestine],...probably...in the last century before our era, and translated soon after." LXX Job used T.Job as a source. "The religious teaching of the book is characteristic of the Hasidim."

1951   Spadafora, F. "Giobbe V: Testamento de G.," in ENCICLOPEDIA CATTOLICA 6, 413f. Jewish, from second century CE.

1958   Philonenko, M. "Le Testament de Job et les Therapeutes," SEMITICA 8, 41-53. Supports Kohler's thesis of a Therapeutic origin by appealing to Qumranic parallels.

1959   Meyer, R. "Hiobstestament," in DIE RELIGION IN GESCHICHTE UND GEGENWART^3 3, 361. T.Job is probably a freely reworked Christian edition of a Hebrew, possibly Essenic, vorlage.

1960   Carstensen, R. THE PERSISTENCE OF THE 'ELIHU' POINT OF VIEW IN LATER JEWISH LITERATURE (unpublished Vanderbilt PhD dissertation), summarized in LEXINGTON THEOLOGICAL QUARTERLY 2 (1967) 37-46. Relies heavily on T.Job material to argue that post-biblical Elihu traditions reflect proto-gnostic interests.

1961   Glatzer, N. THE REST IS COMMENTARY. A SOURCE BOOK OF JUDAIC ANTIQUITY = Beacon Texts in the Judaic Tradition 1 (Beacon, Boston). Chapter 5 contains an abridged English translation of T.Job.

1962   Fritsch, C. "Pseudepigrapha," in INTERPRETERS DICTIONARY OF THE BIBLE 3, 961. Aramaic midrash on Job from first century BCE.

1965   Currie, S. "'Speaking in Tongues,' Early Evidence Outside the NT bearing on 'glossais lalein,'" INTERPRETATION 19, 274-94. Discusses T.Job 48-50 (see also P.Volz, DER GEIST GOTTES... (Mohr, Tubingen, 1910), 132 n.2, etc.).

1965   Hartom, A.S. HA-SEFARIM HA-HISONIM (Tel Aviv) 6, 1-42. Modern Hebrew translation mixing Kohler's verse divisions with James' chapter divisions. More popular in style than Kahana's 1936/37 rendering.

1966   Glatzer, N. "The Book of Job and its Interpreters," in BIBLICAL MOTIFS, ed. A. Altman = Brandeis Studies and Texts 3 (Harvard Univ. Press), 197-220. T.Job is the best documentation of Job pictured as a saint. Hebrew original probably composed in first century BCE.

1966   Philonenko, M. "Hiobs Testament," in BIBLISCH-HISTORISCHES HANDWÖRTERBUCH 2, 726f.

1966   Werblowsky, R.J. and Wigoder, G. "Job, Testament of," in The ENCYCLO-PEDIA OF THE JEWISH RELIGION, 213. "Probably written in answer to the problem of pagan domination."

1967   Brock, S. TESTAMENTUM IOBI (with J.-C. Picard, APOCALYPSIS BARUCHI GRAECE) = Pseudepigrapha Veteris Testamenti graece 2 (Brill, Leiden). Reedits MS P, noting all significant variations in S and V, and selected variants in slav.

1967   Rahnenführer, D. DAS TESTAMENT HIOBS IN SEINEN VARHÄLTNIS ZUM NT (unpublished Halle-Wittenberg Univ. doctoral dissertation). Focuses on lexical correspondences with NT vocabulary. Dates T.Job in late first century BCE.

1967   Urbach, E. "The Traditions about Merkabah Mysticism in the Tannaitic Period" (in Modern Hebrew), in STUDIES IN MYSTICISM AND RELIGION (Festschrift G. Scholem; Magnes, Jerusalem), 1-28. Includes discussion of affinities of T.Job materials with Merkabah mysticism.

1968   Delcor, M. "Le Testament de Job, la prière de Nabonide et les traditions targoumiques," in BIBEL UND QUMRAN, ed. S. Wagner (Evangelische Hauptbibelgesellschaft, Berlin), 54-74. Concludes that the Greek interpolation at Job 2.9 derives from T.Job and that T.Job 17.1 alludes to the invasion of Palestine by Pacorus in 40 BCE, after which T.Job was composed.

1968   Philonenko, M. LE TESTAMENT DE JOB = SEMITICA 18, 1-75. French translation with brief notes and introduction. Original language of T.Job not determined--at least parts come from Hebrew (e.g. ch 43). An authentically Jewish writing of Egyptian Therapeutic origin, from first century CE (pre 70). Also announces existence of the Coptic version.

1969   Glatzer, N. THE DIMENSIONS OF JOB (Schocken). "The Folk Tale Tradition" is traced on pp. 12-16, including T.Job material.

1970   Denis, A.-M. INTRODUCTION AUX PSEUDEPIGRAPHES GRECS D'ANCIEN TESTAMENT = Studia in Veteris Testamenti Pseudepigrapha (Brill, Leiden), 100-105. Summarizes and catalogues previous work.

1971   Spittler, R. THE TESTAMENT OF JOB: INTRODUCTION, TRANSLATION, AND NOTES (unpublished Harvard PhD dissertation). Favors Kohler-Philonenko theory of Therapeutae origin, but also suggests possibility of Montanist redaction around the year 194 CE. Literalistic English translation with full apparatus in English and extensive notes.

1971   Wacholder, B.-Z. "Job, Testament of," in ENCYCLOPAEDIA JUDAICA 10, 129-30. The present Greek text is "closely linked with the Greco-Jewish historian Aristeas...and with the Greek version of Job," and is based on a Hebrew or Aramaic model (from Palestinian-Qumranic background), with later additions and probably also abridgements. No Christian editing is present. Therapeutae produced the Greek form. Referred to in James 5.11.

TESTAMENT OF JOB

TEXT, TRANSLATION, APPARATUS

Διάταξις τοῦ Ἰώβ

(1.1) Βίβλος Ἰὼβ τοῦ καλουμένου Ἰωβάβ

1.1 (2) ἐν ᾗ γὰρ ἡμέρᾳ νοσήσας ἐξετέλει αὐτοῦ τὴν οἰκονομίαν
 (3) ἐκάλεσεν τοὺς ἑπτὰ υἱοὺς αὐτοῦ καὶ τὰς τρεῖς θυγατέρας ὧν
  ἐστὶν τὰ ὀνόματα ταῦτα·
   ⟨Τέρσι, Χορός, Ὕων, Νίκη, Φόρος,⟩ Φίφι, Κρύων, Ἡμέρα,
   Κασσία, Ἀμαλθείας-κέρας.
.2 (4) καλέσας δὲ αὐτοῦ τὰ δέκα τέκνα εἶπεν
  περικυκλώσαντες, τέκνα μου, περικυκλώσατέ με, καὶ ὑποδείξω
  ὑμῖν ἃ ἐποίησεν κύριος μετ' ἐμοῦ καὶ τὰ γενόμενά μοι πάντα.
.3 (5) ἐγὼ γάρ εἰμι ὁ πατὴρ ὑμῶν Ἰὼβ ὁ ἐν πάσῃ ὑπομονῇ γενόμενος,
  ὑμεῖς δὲ γένος ἐκλεκτὸν τίμιον ἐκ σπέρματος Ἰ⟨ακ⟩ὼβ τοῦ
  πατρὸς ⟨τῆς μητρὸς⟩ ὑμῶν.
.4 (6) ἐγὼ γάρ εἰμι ἐκ τῶν υἱῶν Ἠσαῦ ἀδελφὸς Νάωρ
  μητὴρ δὲ ὑμῶν ἐστιν Δίνα ἐξ ἧς ἐγέννησα ὑμᾶς.
  ἡ γὰρ προτέρα μου γυνὴ ἐτελεύτησεν μετὰ ἄλλων δέκα τέκνων
  ἐν πικρῷ θανάτῳ.

.6 Ἀκούσατε οὖν, τέκνα, καὶ δηλώσω ὑμῖν τὰ συμβεβηκότα μοι.
2.1 ἐγὼ γὰρ ἤμην Ἰωβὰβ πρὸ τοῦ ὀνομάσαι με ὁ κύριος Ἰώβ·
.2 ὅτε ἐκαλούμην Ἰωβὰβ ⟨ᾦκε⟩ον τὸ πρὶν ἔγγιστα εἰδωλίου
.3 θρησκευομένου· καὶ συνεχῶς βλέπων ὁλοκαυτώματα αὐτῷ
  ἀναφερόμενα διελογιζόμην ἐν ἑαυτῷ λέγων
(4) ἆρα οὗτός ἐστιν ὁ θεὸς ὁ ποιήσας τὸν οὐρανὸν καὶ τὴν γῆν
  καὶ τὴν θάλασσαν καὶ ἡμᾶς αὐτούς; ἆρα πῶς γνώσομαι;

---

title	So S: Testament (diathēkē) of Job--Book of the words of Job, who is called Jobab P; Testament (diathēkē) of the blameless and severely tested and blessed job--Book of Job, who is called Jobab, both his life and a transcription of his testament (diathēkē) V; Life and career of the holy and righteous Job slav
1.1a	he was - stewardship SP; and having known of his departure from the body V
1.1b-2a	whose names - he said S(P): and said to them Vslav
1.1b	these S: om P
1.1b	⟨Tersi - Phoros⟩P: om S
1.1b	Kryon S: Phrouon P
1.2a	ten S; om P
1.2b	and I will tell S: and listen and I will explain V; so that I may tell P
1.3b	and you are - ⟨grand⟩father (S)P: approved. Know then for yourselves, my children, that you are the race of a chosen one, and preserve your noble lineage V

TESTAMENT OF JOB

(1.1) BOOK OF JOB, WHO IS CALLED JOBAB

1.1a (2) On the day on which, having fallen ill, he was completing his
(3) stewardship, he called his seven sons and three daughters, whose
names are these--

.1b <Tersi, Choros, Hyon, Nike, Phoros>, Phiphe, Kryon,
Hemera, Kassia, (and) Amaltheias-keras.

.2a (4) And when he had called his ten children he said:

.2b Gather round, my children, gather round me, and I will
tell you what the Lord did with me and all the things
that have happened to me.

.3a (5) For I am your father Job, who exhibits complete endurance:

.3b and you are a chosen and honored race from the
seed of J<ac>ob, your <maternal grand>father.

.4a (6) For I am of the sons of Esau, (and) a brother of Nahor;

.4b and your mother is Dinah, from whom I begot you.

.5 (For my former wife died with ten other children in a bitter
death.)

.6 So hear me, children, and I will show you the things which have

2.1 befallen me. Now I was Jobab before the Lord named me Job.

.2 When I was called Jobab, I used to <dwell> quite near a

.3a venerated idol. And as I continually saw whole-burnt offerings
being offered up to it, I was debating within myself saying:

.3b (4) Can this be the God who made heaven and earth and
the sea and our very selves? How then shall I know?

1.3b   Jacob - <grand>father P: Job your father Sslav
1.4a   Esau, (and) [I am] a brother of Nahor Vslav: Esau, [who is] a
       brother of Nahor S; Esau, [who is] a brother of Jacob P; Esau, a
       brother of Jacob, and I am a brother of Nahor cj Kraft
1.4b   and your (our V) mother SVslav: (Jacob) of whom is your mother P
1.6   children SV: my children P
2.1   I was (eimen [=V]; eimi [lit. "am"] SP) Jobab SP: I was rich,
       exceeding eastern (rulers), in the region Ausitis and V
2.2   when P: then (tote) S: om V
2.2   I used to <dwell> - idol P: being (on) - idol S; and the beginning
       of my trial occurred as follows: for neighboring my house was a
       certain idol of one worshipped by the people V; formerly I
       worshipped idols slav
2.3a   to it SP: + as to (a) God V
2.3b   our very selves SP: all of us V; all that is in them slav
2.3b   know SP: + the truth V

TESTAMENT OF JOB

3.1   καὶ ἐν τῇ νυκτὶ κοιμωμένου μου ἦλθέν μοι φωνὴ μεγάλη,
           φωνὴ ἐν μείζονι φωτὶ λέγουσα
           Ἰωβάβ Ἰωβάβ.
.2   καὶ ἐγὼ εἶπον
           ἰδοὺ ἐγώ.
.3   καὶ εἶπεν
           ἀνάστηθι καὶ ὑποδείξω σοι τίς ἐστιν οὗτος ὃν γνῶναι θέλεις.
.4   (3)   οὗτος ᾧ τὰ ὁλοκαυτώματα προσφέρονται καὶ ᾧ σπένδουσιν
           οὐκ ἔστιν θεὸς ἀλλὰ αὕτη ἐστὶν ἡ δύναμις τοῦ διαβόλου
           ἐν ᾗ ἀπατηθήσεται ἡ ἀνθρωπίνη φύσις.
.5   (4)   καὶ ἐγὼ ἀκούσας κατέπεσα ἐπὶ τὴν κλίνην μου προσκυνῶν καὶ
           λέγων
     (5)   κύριέ μου ὁ ἐπὶ σωτηρίᾳ τῆς ἐμῆς ψυχῆς ἐλθών,
     (6)   δέομαί σου, εἴπερ οὗτός ἐστιν ὁ τόπος τοῦ Σατανᾶ ἐν ᾧ
           ἀπατηθήσονται οἱ ἄνθρωποι, δός μοι ἐξουσίαν ἵνα ἀπελθὼν
     (7)   καθαρίσω αὐτοῦ τὸν τόπον ἵνα μηκέτι ποιήσωμεν σπένδεσθαι
           αὐτόν.
.6   καὶ τίς ἐστιν ὁ κωλύων με βασιλεύοντα ταύτης τῆς χώρας;
4.1   καὶ ἀποκριθεὶς μοι τὸ φῶς εἶπεν ὅτι
           μὲν καθαρίσαι τούτου τὸν ναὸν δυνήσῃ--τι ὅτι μέλλει
.2   ἐνεργῆσαι τοῦ ἀνοικοδωμῆσαι αὐτόν; ἀλλὰ ἰδοὺ ὑποδείκνυμί
           σοι πάντα ἅπερ ἐνετείλατό μοι ὁ κύριος μεταδιδόναι σοι.
.3   (2)   κἀγὼ εἶπον ὅτι
           πάντα ὅσα ἐντελεῖται τῷ θεράποντι αὐτοῦ ἀκούσομαι καὶ πράξω.
.4   (3)   καὶ πάλιν εἶπεν
           τάδε λέγει κύριος·
     (4)   ἀπόλεσαι ἐὰν ἐπιχειρήσῃς καὶ καθαίρῃς τὸν τόπον τοῦ
           Σατανᾶ, ἀναστήσεταί σοι μετὰ ὀργῆς εἰς πόλεμον, εἰ μὴ
.5   μόνον θάνατόν σοι οὐ δυνήσεται προσενεγκεῖν. ἐπιφέρει
     (5)   δέ σοι πολλὰς πληγὰς καὶ ἀφαιρεῖταί σοι πάντα τὰ

3.1a   the night SP: that night V
3.1a   loud SP: om V
3.1a   a voice S: om PV
3.2a-3a   And I said - and he said SP: om V
3.4b   power SP: + and work V
3.4b   by which SV: by whom P
3.4b   human nature SP: man V
3.5a   heard SP: + these things V
3.5a   on my bed SP: to the earth V
3.5b   came SP: speaks to me V
3.5b   in which - libations to him SP: I beg you command me to go and
         obliterate him/it and purge this place V
3.6   since - region SP: to do so since I am king of this region so
         those in it are no longer deceived V
4.1a   light SP: voice from the light V
4.1b   the temple of this one S: this place P; the place V

3.1a	And in the night as I was sleeping a loud voice came to me, a voice in a great light saying,
.1b	Jobab, Jobab!
.2a	And I said,
.2b	Behold it is I.
.3a (2b)	And he said:
.3b	Arise, and I shall tell you who this is whom you wish to know.
.4a (3)	This one to whom they bring whole-burnt offerings and to whom
.4b	they pour out libations is not God, but this is the power of the devil by which human nature is deceived.
.5a (4)	And when I heard, I fell on my bed worshipping and saying:
.5b (5)	My Lord, who came for the salvation of my soul,
(6)	I beg you, if this is indeed the place of Satan in which men are deceived, grant me authority to go and purge
(7)	his place so that we no longer make libations to him.
.6	And who is the one who forbids me, since I rule this region?
4.1a	And the light answered me and said:
.1b	You will be able to purge the temple of this one--why would he
.2	take action to rebuild it? But behold, I am going to tell you all the things which the Lord commanded me to communicate to you.
.3a (2)	And I said,
.3b	Whatever he commands his servant, I shall hear and do.
.4a (3)	And again he said,
.4b	Thus says the Lord:
.4c (4)	If you attempt to destroy and you purge the place of Satan, he will angrily rise against you for battle, except that he will not be able to bring death upon you.
.5	But he will inflict many misfortunes on you and he will take
(5)	away all your possessions; he will carry off your servants.

4.1b why - rebuild it S: om PV [the phrase is difficult and awkward: for ti hoti, cj Mancini dioti (wherefore), cj Kraft tis te/de (and who); for "he" perhaps "you" (melleis); for "rebuild" perhaps "repay" (antapodosai); it need not be a question--"wherefore he/you will", etc.]
4.2 behold SV: om P
4.2 to communicate to you SP: to say to you, for I am the archangel of God V
4.4a he said SP: the archangel said to me V
4.4c to destroy SV: om P
4.4c he will PV: pr for S
4.4c except - upon you S(P): and will display in you all his evil V
4.5 misfortunes (or "plagues," diseases") SP: + and hardships V
4.5 all SVslav: om P
4.5 servants (or "children") SP: + and he will do many evils to you, and you will be as an athlete who spars and endures pains and receives the reward and suffers the trials and tribulations V (see 4.8)

.6   ὑπάρχοντα, τὰ παιδία σου ἀναιρεῖ· ἀλλ'ἐὰν ὑπομείνῃς
           ποιήσω σου τὸ ὄνομα ὀνομαστὸν ἐν πάσαις ταῖς γενεαῖς τῆς
           γῆς ἄχρι τῆς συντελείας τοῦ αἰωνός.
.7   καὶ πάλιν ἐπανακάμψω σε ἐπὶ τὰ ὑπάρχοντά σου καὶ
    (8)   ἀποδοθήσεται σοι διπλάσιον ἵνα γνῷς ὅτι ἀπροσωπόληπτός
           ἐστιν ὁ κύριος, ἀποδιδοὺς ἑκάστῳ τῷ ὑπακούοντι ἀγαθά.
.8 (9-10) καὶ ἐγερθήσῃ ἐν τῇ ἀναστάσει καὶ ἔσῃ ὡς ἀθλητὴς πυκτεύων
           καὶ καρτερῶν πόνους καὶ ἐκδεχόμενος τὸν στέφανον.
.9 (11)   τότε γνώσει ὅτι δίκαιος καὶ ἀληθὴς καὶ ἰσχυρὸς ὁ κύριος,
           ἐνισχύων τοὺς ἐκλεκτοὺς αὐτοῦ.
5.1   καὶ ἐγώ, τέκνα μου, ἀνταπεκρίθην αὐτῷ ὅτι
           ἄχρι θανάτου ὑπομενῶ καὶ οὐ μὴ ἀναποδίσω.
.2   καὶ μετὰ τὸ σφραγισθῆναί με ὑπὸ τοῦ ἀγγέλου καὶ ἀπελθόντος
           ἀπ'ἐμοῦ τότε κἀγώ, τέκνα μου, ἀναστὰς ἐν τῇ ἐξῆς νυκτί
           παρέλαβον μεθ' ἑαυτοῦ πεντήκοντα παῖδας καὶ εἰς τὸν ναὸν
           τοῦ εἰδωλίου εἰσελθὼν κατήνεγκα αὐτὸ εἰς τὸ ἔδαφος.
.3   καὶ οὕτως ἀνεχώρησα εἰς τὸν οἶκόν μου κελεύσας ἀσφαλισθῆναι
           τὰς θύρας.

6.1-.2   Ἀκούσατε, τέκνα, καὶ θαυμάσατε. ἅμα τε γὰρ εἰσῆλθον εἰς
           τὸν οἶκόν μου καὶ τὰς θύρας μου ἠσφάλισα ἐνετειλάμην τοῖς
           προθύροις μου ὅτι
    (3)   εἴ τις σήμερον ζητήσῃ με μὴ σημανθήτω μοι
           ἀλλὰ εἴπατε ὅτι
           οὐ σχολάζει· περὶ πράγματος ἀναγκαίου ἔνδον ἐστίν.
.3 (4)   καὶ ἐμοῦ ἔνδος ὄντος, ὁ Σατανᾶς μετασχηματισθεὶς εἰς
   (5)   ἐπαίτην ἔκρουσεν τῇ θύρᾳ λέγων τῇ θυρωρῷ
           σήμανον τῷ Ἰὼβ λέγουσα ὅτι
           βούλομαι συντυχεῖν σοι.
.4 (6-7)   καὶ ἡ θυρωρὸς ἐλθοῦσα λέγει μοι ταῦτα καὶ ἤκουσεν παρ'
           ἐμοῦ δηλῶσαι μὴ νῦν μοι σχολάζειν.

4.7   double payment SP: + of all that you lost V
4.7   the Lord S: God V; he P
4.7   obedient SP: + which shall also be given to you, and you will
        receive an unfading crown V
4.8a resurrection SP: + to eternal life V
4.8b and (for P) you will be like - crown SP: om V (see 4.5)
4.9   giving-ones SP: om V
5.1b endure SP: + everything that happens to me, for the sake of the
        love of God V
5.2   And after - children SP: then the angel departed from me after
        having sealed me V
5.2   I razed SP: I destroyed V

.6   But if you endure, I shall make your name renowned
             in all earthly generations until the consummation of the age.
.7   And I shall restore you once again to your possessions
   (8)   and you will receive a double payment, so that you may know
             that the Lord is impartial, rendering good things to each one
.8a (9)   who is obedient. And you will be raised up in the resurrection
.8b (10)   and you will be like an athlete who spars and endures hard
.9 (11)   labors and wins the crown. Then you will know that the Lord
             is just, true, and strong--giving strength to his elect ones.
5.1a   And I, my children, replied to him:
.1b   Till death I will endure and I will not retreat.
.2   And after I had been sealed by the angel and he departed from me,
             then, I, my children, having arisen the next night took with me
             fifty servants and entering the temple of the idol,
.3   I razed it to the ground. And so I withdrew into my house,
             after ordering the doors to be secured.
6.1/.2a   Hear, children, and marvel. For as soon as I entered my house
             and secured my doors, I commanded my doormen,
.2b (3)   If anyone seeks me today, don't inform me but say,
.2c   He has no time; he is inside concerned with an urgent matter.
.3a (4)   And while I was inside, Satan knocked at the door, having
   (5)   disguised himself as a beggar, and said to the doormaid,
.3b   Inform Job by saying,
.3c   I wish to meet with you.
.4a (6)   And when the doormaid came, she told me these things
.4b (7)   and was told to report that I had no time now.

6.1-.2a   Hear (+ me P) - doors SP; om V
6.2b   but say SP: + to him Vslav
6.2c   has no time SP: is concentrating/studying (same verb, without
            negative; see 6.4b) V
6.2c   urgent matters V
6.3a   and - inside SP: then V
6.3c   you SP: him V
6.4b   to report - now SP: I am **concentrating/studying** (see 6.2c) V

7.1		Ὁ δὲ Σατανᾶς ἀπῆλθεν καὶ ἔθετο τοῖς ὤμοις αὐτοῦ ἀσσάλιον
.2		καὶ ἐλθὼν λελάληκεν τῇ θυρωρῷ λέγων
	(2)	εἶπον τῷ Ιωβ .
		δός μοι ἄρτον ἐκ τῶν χειρῶν σου ἵνα φάγω.
.3		καὶ ἐγὼ ἄρτον κεκαυμένον δέδωκα τῇ παιδὶ δοῦναι αὐτῷ
.4		καὶ ἐδήλωσα ⟨αὐτῇ εἰπεῖν⟩ αὐτῷ ὅτι
	(4)	μηκέτι προσδόκα φαγεῖν ἐκ τῶν ἐμῶν ἄρτων, ὅτι ἀπηλλοτριώθην σοι.
.5		καὶ ἡ θυρωρὸς αἰδεσθεῖσα ἐπιδοῦναι αὐτῷ τὸν κεκαυμένον
	(6)	ἄρτον καὶ σποδοειδῆ ἐπεὶ μὴ ἔγνωκεν αὐτὸν εἶναι τὸν Σατανᾶν
.6	(7)	ἦρεν ἐκ τῶν ἑαυτῆς ἄρτον καλὸν καὶ ἔδωκεν αὐτῷ. ὁ δὲ λαβὼν καὶ γνοὺς τὸ γεγονός εἶπεν τῇ παιδί
		ἀπελθοῦσα, κακὴ δούλη, φέρε μοι τὸν δοθέντα σοι δοθῆναί μοι ἄρτον.
.7	(8)	καὶ ἔκλαυσεν μετὰ λύπης μεγάλης ⟨ἡ παῖς⟩ λέγουσα ἀληθῶς καλῶς λέγεις εἶναί με κακὴν δούλην,
	(9)	ὅτι οὐκ ἐποίησα καθῶς προσετάχθη μοι ὑπὸ τοῦ δεσπότου μου.
.8		καὶ ὑποστρέψασα προσήνεγκεν τὸν κεκαυμένον ἄρτον λέγουσα αὐτῷ
		τάδε λέγει ὁ κύριός μου ὅτι
	(10)	οὐ μὴ φάγῃς ἐκ τῶν ἄρτων μου ἔτι, διότι ἀπηλλοτριώθην σου.
.9	(11)	ἀκμὴν καὶ τοῦτό σοι ἔδωκα ἵνα μὴ ἐγκληθῶ ὅτι τῷ αἰτήσαντι ἐχθρῷ οὐδὲν παρέσχον.
.10	(12)	καὶ ταῦτα ἀκούσας ὁ Σατανᾶς ἀντέπεμψέν μοι τὴν παῖδα λέγων ὅτι
		ὡς ὁλόκαυστός ἐστιν ὁ ἄρτος οὗτος, οὕτως ποιήσω καὶ
.11		τὸ σῶμά σου τοιοῦτον· ἐν γὰρ μιᾷ ὥρᾳ ἀπέρχομαι καὶ ἐρημώσω σε.
.12	(13)	καὶ ἀνταπεκρίθην αὐτῷ
.13		ὃ ποιεῖς ποίησον, οἵα βούλῃ ἀγωγῇ· ἕτοιμος γάρ εἰμι ὑποστῆναι ἅπερ φέρεις μοι.

7.1   And Satan (+ having heard P) SP: Failing in this, the evil one V
7.1   <u>assalion</u> (+ ragged/tattered/wrinkled V) SPV--the meaning is unclear; conjectures include "yoke" (see gk <u>asilla</u>), "garment" (so V: see gk <u>attalianon</u>; lat <u>axilla</u> = "winged," perhaps describing a garment or wallet [so Lampe, <u>Lex</u>, sv]), "basket" (see semitic <u>sal</u>, <u>asiyla</u>). Perhaps also worth consideration are "wineskin/bag made of skin" (gk askos, dim askidion) or "small shield" (gk <u>aspidion</u>).
7.3   And I P: + Job S; + hearing these things V
7.4a   I told ⟨her to say⟩ cj Kraft (or "I ⟨said to her to⟩ tell him"): I told SV; I said P
7.4b   I have become...to you SV (see 7.8): you have become...to me P
7.5   a (one P) good loaf from her own SP: from her good loaves V
7.6b   bring me SVslav: bring P

7.1		And Satan departed and put an <u>assalion</u> on his shoulders.
.2a		And when he came, he spoke to the doormaid saying:
.2b	(2)	Say to Job,
		Give me a loaf of bread from your hands so I may eat.
.3		And I gave the girl a burnt loaf to give to him.
.4a		And I told <her to say> to him:
.4b	(4)	Don't expect to eat from my loaves any longer, for I have become a stranger to you.
.5		And the doormaid, ashamed to give him the burnt and ashen loaf,
	(6)	since she did not know he was Satan, took a good
.6a	(7)	loaf from her own and gave it to him. But when he received it, and since he knew what had occurred, he said to the girl:
.6b		Away with you, evil servant, bring me the loaf which was given you to be given to me.
.7a	(8)	And <the girl> wept with deep grief saying:
.7b		You quite properly say that I am an evil servant, since
	(9)	I did not do just as I was instructed by my master.
.8a		And when she returned she brought the burnt loaf, saying to him:
.8b		Thus says my lord:
.8c	(10)	You shall not eat from my loaves any longer, for I have become
.9	(11)	a stranger to you. Yet I have just now given this one to you in order that I may not be accused of providing nothing to an enemy who makes a request.
.10a	(12)	And when he heard these things Satan sent the girl back to me saying:
.10b		As this loaf is wholly burnt, so I shall also make your
.11		body. For within one hour I am going to depart and I will make you desolate.
.12a	(13)	And I replied to him:
.12b		Do what you are going to do, whatever you plan to bring about.
.13		For I am prepared to undergo whatever you inflict on me.

7.7a	<the girl> PV: om S
7.7a	deep SP: om V
7.7b	properly SPslav: om V
7.7b	since I did not SV: for if I were not, I would P
7.8a	brought S: + him PV
7.10a	and SV: om P
7.10b	as - burnt SP: as you see this wholly burnt loaf V
7.10b	make SP: pr speedily V
7.11	om entire verse V
7.12b	whatever - bring about (+ make happen V) SV: For if you wish to bring something upon me P
7.13	For SV: om P (see 7.12)

8.1 (1-2) Ὅτε δὲ ἀπέστη ἀπ' ἐμοῦ, ἀπελθὼν ὑπὸ τὸ στερέωμα ὥρμωσεν
.2 (3)   τὸν κύριον ἵνα λάβῃ ἐξουσίαν κατὰ τῶν ὑπαρχόντων μοι. καὶ
          τότε λαβὼν τὴν ἐξουσίαν κατὰ τῶν ὑπαρχόντων μοι ἦλθεν καὶ
          ἦρέν μου τὸν σύμπαντα πλοῦτον.

9.1   Ἀκούσατε οὖν καὶ ὑποδείξω ὑμῖν πάντα τὰ συμβεβηκότα μοι
          καὶ τὰ ἀρθέντα μοι.

.2   εἶχον γὰρ ἑκατὸν τριάκοντα χιλιάδας προβάτων,
   (3)   καὶ ἀφώρισα ἀπ' αὐτῶν χιλιάδας ἑπτὰ καρῆναι εἰς ἔνδυσιν
          ὀρφανῶν καὶ χηρῶν καὶ πενήτων καὶ ἀδυνάτων·

.3   Ἦν δέ μοι ἀγέλη κυνῶν ὀκτακόσιοι, οἳ ἐφύλασσόν μοι τὰ
          ποίμνια· εἶχον δὲ καὶ ἄλλους διακοσίους κύνας φυλάσσοντας
          τὸν οἶκον.

.4   εἶχον δὲ καμήλους ἐννακισχιλίους,
          καὶ ἐξ αὐτῶν ἐποδισάμην τρισχιλίους ἐργάζεσθαι κατὰ πᾶσαν
   (5)   πόλιν, καὶ γομώσας ἀγαθῶν ἀπέστελλον εἰς τὰς πόλεις καὶ εἰς
          τὰς κώμας ἐντελλόμενος ἀπελθεῖν καὶ ταῖς χηραῖς.

.5 (6)   εἶχον δὲ ἑκατὸν τεσσαράκοντα χιλιάδας ὄνων νομάδων καὶ
          ἐξ αὐτῶν ἀφώρισα πεντακοσίους, καὶ τὴν ἐξ αὐτῶν γονὴν
          ἐκέλευον πιπράσκεσθαι καὶ διδόναι τοῖς πένησιν καὶ
          ἐπιδεομένοις.

.6 (7)   Καὶ ἤρχοντό μοι εἰς ἀπάντησιν ἀπὸ πασῶν τῶν χωρῶν ἅπαντες.
.7   ἀνεῳγμέναι δὲ ἦσαν αἱ τέσσαρες θύραι τοῦ οἴκου μου.
.8   ἐκέλευον δὲ τοῖς οἰκέταις μου ταύτας εἶναι ἀνεῳγμένας τοῦτο
          σκοπῶν μὴ ἄρα ἔλθωσίν τινες ἐλεημοσύνην ζητοῦντες καὶ
          ἴδωσίν με παρακαθεζόμενον ⟨τῇ θύρᾳ καὶ αἰδεσθέντες ἀποστραφῶσιν
.9   μηδὲν λαβόντες· ἀλλ' ὅταν ἴδωσίν με πρὸς μίαν θύραν καθήμενον⟩
          δυνηθῶσιν διὰ τῆς ἄλλης ἀπελθεῖν καὶ λαβεῖν ὅσον χρῄζουσιν.

8.1   But after SP: When the devil heard these things V
8.1   when SP: pr and V
8.2   then SP: om P
8.2   over my possessions S; om P; from God V
8.2   took SP: pr immediately V
9.1   om entire verse V
9.1   and I S: for I P
9.2b sheared SP: om V
9.3   flocks - guarding the SV: om P
9.4b and I - them SP: om V
9.4b hobbled the feet cj Kraft: epolesamēn S (epōl- ? "foaled" or
      "sold" ?); selected P (see 10.5b)

8.1 (2)   But after he withdrew from me, when he had gone out under the
          firmament, he implored the Lord that he might receive authority over
.2 (3)   my possessions. And then when he had received the authority over
          my possessions, he came and took away all my wealth.

9.1   Listen then and I will show you all the things which have
          befallen me and the things which have been taken from me.

.2a   For I used to have 130,000 sheep,
.2b (3)   and I set aside 7000 of them to be sheared for the clothing
          of orphans and widows, and poor and helpless.

.3a   And I had a pack of 80 dogs which guarded my flocks,
.3b   and I also had 200 other dogs guarding the house.

.4a   And I used to have 9000 camels,
.4b   and I hobbled the feet of 3000 of them to work in every city;
.4c (5)   and after I loaded them with good things, I sent them into
          the cities and into the villages, commanding that they depart and
          distribute to the helpless and to the unfortunate and to the widows.

.5a (6)   And I used to have 140,000 grazing she-asses,
.5b   and I set aside 500 of them and gave a standing order for their
          offspring to be sold and given to the poor and the needy.

.6 (7)   And everyone from all regions began coming to meet me.
.7   And the four doors of my house were open.
.8   And I would command my house servants that the doors be open,
          since I was concerned lest anyone come seeking alms and see
          me sitting at <the door and turn back ashamed, having
.9   taken nothing. But whenever they saw me sitting at one door>
          they could exit through the other and take as much as they
          might need.

9.4c   and after - with SP: to carry loads of V
9.4c   the cities SP: every city V (see 9.4b)
9.4c   commanding - distribute SP: om V
9.4c   unfortunate and...(+ all P) widows SP: sickly and...needy V
9.5a   140,000 SVslav: 130,000 P (see 9.2a)
9.5b   given SP: the income to be given V
9.6   And everyone SP: For the poor V
9.7   And SP: For V
9.8   And I - open SP: om V
9.8   seeking SV: asking P
9.8-.9 <the door - one door> P: one of the doors V: om S
9.9   exit SVslav: enter P

10.1 Ἦσαν δέ μοι καὶ τράπεζαι ἰδρυμέναι τριάκοντα ἐν τῷ οἴκῳ μου
.2 ἀκίνητοι πάσας ὥρας τοῖς ξένοις μόνοις· εἶχον δὲ καὶ τῶν
.3 χηρῶν δώδεκα τραπέζας κειμένας. καὶ εἴ τις ξένος ἤρχετο
αἰτῶν ἐλεημοσύνην, ἀνάγκην εἶχεν τρέφεσθαι ἐν τῇ τραπέζῃ
.4 πρὶν λαβεῖν τὴν χρείαν· καὶ οὐδὲ ἐπέτρεπον ἐξελθεῖν τὴν
θύραν μου κόλπῳ κενῷ·

.5 εἶχον δὲ τρισχίλια πεντακόσια ζεύγη βοῶν,
καὶ ἐξελεξάμην ἐξ αὐτῶν πεντακόσια καὶ ἔταξα εἰς τὸν
ἀροτριασμόν, ὃν δύνανται ποιεῖν ἐν τῷ παντὶ ἀγρῷ τῶν
(6) προσλαμβανόντων αὐ<τά, καὶ> τῶν καρπῶν αὐτῶν ἀφώριζον
τοῖς πένησιν εἰς τὴν τράπεζαν αὐτῶν.

.6 (7) εἶχον δὲ ἀρτοκόπια πεντήκοντα ἀφ' ὧν ἔταξα εἰς τὴν ὑπηρεσίαν
τῇ τῶν πτωχῶν τραπέζῃ.

11.1 Ἦσαν δὲ καὶ ξένοι <τινὲς> ἰδόντες τὴν ἐμὴν προθυμίαν καὶ
.2 ἐπεθύμησαν καὶ αὐτοὶ ὑπηρετῆσαι τῇ διακονίᾳ. καὶ ἄλλοι
τινὲς ἦσάν ποτε ἀποροῦντες, καὶ μηδὲν δυνάμενοι ἀναλῶσαι·
.3 καὶ ἤρχοντο παρακαλοῦντες καὶ λέγοντες
δεόμεθά σου ἐπειδὴ καὶ ἡμεῖς δυνάμεθα ταύτην ἐκτελέσαι <τὴν>
(3) διακονίαν καὶ οὐδὲν κεκτήμεθα, ποίησον σὺ μεθ' ἡμῶν ἔλεος
καὶ προχείρησον ἡμῖν χρυσίον ἵνα ἀπέλθωμεν εἰς τὰς μακρὰς
πόλεις καὶ ἐμπορευσάμενοι τοῖς πένησιν δυνηθῶμεν ποιήσασθαι
.4 διακονίαν· καὶ μετὰ τοῦτο ἀποκαταστήσωμέν σοι τὸ ἴδιον σου.
.5 καὶ ἐγὼ ταῦτα ἀκούων ἠγαλλιώμην ὅτι ὅλως παρ' ἐμοῦ
.6 λαμβάνουσιν εἰς οἰκονομίαν τῶν πτωχῶν· καὶ προθύμως
(7) δεξάμενος τὸ γραμματεῖον ἐδίδουν αὐτοῖς ὅσον ἤθελον, μὴ
λαμβάνων παρ' αὐτῶν ἐνέχυρα εἰ μὴ μόνον ἔγγραφον.
.7 (8) καὶ οὕτως ἐπορεύοντο ἐν τοῖς ἐμοῖς.

10.1	in my house SP: om V
10.2	twelve SV: + other P
10.3	any stranger SP: anyone V
10.4	stomach: possibly "pocket" (fold or hollow of robe)
10.5b	500 SV: + yoke P (see 16.1)
10.5b	assigned them S(P): + all V
10.5b	which they could do SP: om V
10.5c	<and> PV: om S
10.5c	their produce (pl.) S (P sing.): the revenue from their produce (pl.) V
10.6	assigned SV: + twelve P
10.6	the ministry of SP: om Vslav
10.6	indigent SP: + and I used to have special servants for this ministry V

10.1		And I had thirty special tables in my house reserved at
	.2	all hours for strangers only. And I also used to have twelve
	.3	tables set for the widows. And if any stranger approached to ask alms, he was required to take nourishment at table before
	.4	receiving his request. Nor would I permit him to depart from my door with an empty stomach.
	.5a	And I used to have 3500 yoke of oxen,
	.5b	and I chose from them 500 and assigned them for ploughing, which they could to do in every field of those who made use of them,
	.5c (6)	<and> I set apart their produce for the poor, for their table.
	.6 (7)	And I used to have fifty bakeries from which I assigned for the ministry of the table of the indigent.
11.1		And there were also <certain> strangers who saw my zeal,
	.2	and they also desired to assist in the service. And there were certain others at that time without resources and unable to spend a
	.3a	thing. And they came urging me, saying:
	.3b	We beg you, since we could also engage in this service, but
	(3)	own nothing, show mercy on us and furnish us money so we may depart for distant cities and by engaging in trade we can do the poor a service.
	.4	And after this we shall restore to you what is your own.
	.5	And when I heard these things I would rejoice that they would
	.6	take anything at all from me for the care of the indigent. And accepting the note eagerly, I would give them as much as they
	(7)	wished--not taking from them any security except only a
	.7 (8)	written note. And so they would go with my resources.

11.1	<certain> PV: om S
11.2	at that time SP: om V
11.3a	And S: om PV
11.3b	since SV: om Pslav
11.3b	furnish SV: lend (<u>prochrēson</u>) P
11.3b	and by engaging in trade S: to trade and P; + and an abundance of commerce V
11.5	these PV: such (<u>toiauta</u>) S
11.6	as much: or perhaps, "as long" (see 11.10b)
11.7	so SP: as they went V
11.7	go SV: trade (<u>eneporeuonto</u>) P
11.7-9	with my - robbed SP: and give to the poor. Many times certain ones would suffer loss of goods on the road or at sea or would be robbed of them V

.8 (9) ἐνίοτε δὲ ἐμπορευόμενοι ἐπετύγχανον καὶ ἐδίδουν τοῖς πτωχοῖς.
.9 (10) ἐνίοτε δὲ πάλιν ἀπεσυλοῦντο καὶ ἤρχοντο καὶ παρεκάλουν με λέγοντες
  δεόμεθά σου μακροθύμησαν ἐφ' ἡμᾶς ἵνα ἴδωμεν πῶς ἀποκαταστήσωμέν σοι τὰ σά.
.10(11) κἀγὼ ἀνυπερθέτως προέφερον αὐτῶν τὸ χειρόγραφον καὶ ἀνεγίνωσκον στέφανον ἐπιφερόμενος ἀφαιρήσεως λέγων οὕτως
  ὅσον προφάσει τῶν πενήτων ἐπίστευσα ὑμῖν, οὐδὲν λήψομαι παρ' ὑμῶν.
.11(12) καὶ οὐδὲν ἐδεχόμην παρὰ τοῦ ὀφειλέτου μου.

12.1 Καὶ εἴ ποτέ μοι ἤρχετο ἀνὴρ ἱλαρὸς τῇ καρδίᾳ λέγων
  οὐδὲν ἐγὼ εὐπορῶ ἐπικουρῆσαι τοῖς πένησιν·
.2 βούλομαι μέντοι κἂν διακονῆσαι τοῖς πτωχοῖς ἐν τῇ σῇ τραπέζῃ.
.3-.4(2) καὶ συγχωρηθεὶς ὑπηρέτει καὶ ἤσθιεν· καὶ ἑσπέρας γινομένης
.5 ἐξερχόμενος εἰς τὸν οἶκον αὐτοῦ ἐλάμβανεν μισθόν· καὶ εἰ μὴ ἐβούλετο λαβεῖν ἠναγκάζετο παρ' ἐμοῦ λέγοντος
(3) ἐπίσταμαι ὅτι ἐργάτης εἶ ἄνθρωπος προσδοκῶν καὶ ἀναμένων σου τὸν μισθόν, καὶ ἀνάγκην ἔχεις λαβεῖν.
.6 (4) καὶ οὐκ ἔων ⟨μισθὸν⟩ μισθωτοῦ ἀπομένειν παρ' ἐμοὶ ἐν τῇ οἰκίᾳ μου.

13.1 Διεφώνουν δὲ οἱ ἀμέλγοντες τὰς βόας ῥέοντος τοῦ γάλακτος ἐν
(2) τοῖς ὄρεσιν, καὶ τὸ βούτυρον διεχεῖτο ἐν ταῖς ὁδοῖς μου ἀπὸ
.2 τοῦ πλήθους· ἐν ταῖς πέτραις καὶ τοῖς ὄρεσιν ἐκοιτάζοντο διὰ
.3 τὰ λοχευόμενα. καὶ διὰ τοῦτο τὰ μὲν ὄρη ἐκβλύζοντο γάλακτι
.4 καὶ ὡς πεπηγμένον βούτυρον γένεσθαι. ἀπέκαμνον δὲ οἱ δοῦλοί ⟨μου⟩ οἱ τὰ τῶν χηρῶν καὶ τῶν πενήτων ἐδέσματα ἐνέχοντες·

11.9b so that SV: om P
11.9b what is yours SV: om P
11.10a without delay SP: hearing these things and sympathizing with them V
11.10a their note SV: the note to them P
11.10a crowning - cancellation (or perhaps "postponement") SP:
  in their presence and by tearing it up I would release them from obligation V
11.10a thus SVslav: om P
11.10b as long: perhaps "as much" (see 11.6)
11.11 and - nothing SV: nor would I accept anything P
12.2 indigent SV: + today P
12.4 as he was about to leave (+ to depart P) - he received (to receive P) recompense SP: his pay/recompense was given him and he would go to his house rejoicing V
12.5a and if - take it SV: om P

.8	(9)	And sometimes they would be successful trading and would
.9	(10)	give to the indigent. But at other times they **would be robbed**, **and they would come and urge me saying**:
.9b		We beg you, be patient with us so that we may see how we can repay you what is yours.
.10a	(11)	And without delay I would bring forth their note and **read it**, crowning the transaction with **cancellation** by speaking thus:
.10b		As long as I trusted you in the interests of the poor, I will take nothing from you.
.11	(12)	And I would accept nothing from my debtor.
12.1a		And if a man cheerful in heart ever would come to me saying:
.1b		I have nothing available to help the poor.
.2		Nevertheless I wish at least to serve the indigent **at your table**.
.3/.4	(2)	And when he received permission, he would serve and eat. And when it was evening, as he was about to leave for his house, he received
.5a		recompense. And if he did not want to take it, he was compelled by me, saying:
.5b	(3)	I know that you are a workingman who expects and awaits your wage, and you must take it!
.6	(4)	And I did not allow the wage earner's <pay> to remain behind with me in my house.
13.1a		And those who milked the cows were at a loss, since milk
.1b	(2)	flowed on the mountains, and butter spread over my roads from its
.2		abundance. They bedded down in the rocks and in the mountains on
.3		account of the young being born. And because of this, the mountains
.4		were gushing milk and became as congealed butter. And <my> servants, who were in charge of the food of the widows and the poor, grew tired.

12.5a	saying SP: + to him V
12.6	allow - <pay> (om S) SP: once fail to supply recompense/pay for the wage earner or any other, nor did I permit his pay V
12.6	house SP: + a single night V
13.1	were at a loss (or, "would desert") - my roads S(P): or also the ewes would desert the travelers in the road so that they might obtain a share of it, and milk spread its butter on the mountains and in the roads V [see also above, p.8]
13.2	They (the milkers? the cattle?) SV: and my cattle P
13.3	And because of this (these things P) - butter SP: om V
13.3	gushing S: coated with (or "surged with") P
13.4	<my> PV: om S
13.4	were in charge of SV: cooked P
13.4	and the poor SV: om P (see 13.5)
13.4	grew tired: or perhaps "quit" (see 13.1)

.5 καὶ ὀλιγωροῦντες κατηρῶντό μοι λέγοντες
τίς ἂν δῴη ἡμῖν ἐκ τῶν σαρκῶν αὐτοῦ ἐμπλησθῆναι;
.6 λίαν μου χρηστοῦ ὄντος.

14.1 εἶχον δὲ ἐξ ψαλμοὺς καὶ δεκάχορδον κιθάραν·
.2 καὶ διεγειρόμην τὸ καθ' ἡμέραν μετὰ τὸ τρέφεσθαι τὰς χήρας
καὶ ἐλάμβανον τὴν κιθάραν καὶ ἔψαλλον αὐτοῖς, καὶ αὐταὶ
.3 ὕμνουν. καὶ ἐκ τοῦ ψαλτηρίου ἀνεμίμνησκον αὐτὰς τοῦ θεοῦ
.4 ἵνα δοξάσωσιν τὸν κύριον. καὶ εἴ ποτε ἐγόγγυζον αἱ
θεράπαιναί μου, ἐλάμβανον τὸ ψαλτήριον καὶ τὸν μισθὸν τῆς
.5 ἀνταποδόσιας ἔψαλλον αὐταῖς· καὶ κατέπαυον αὐτὰς τῆς ὀλιγωρίας
τοῦ γογγυσμοῦ.

15.1 Καὶ τὰ ἐμὰ τέκνα μετὰ τὴν ὑπηρεσίαν τῆς διακονίας ᾖρον καθ'
.2 ἡμέραν τὸ δεῖπνον αὐτῶν· καὶ εἰσήρχοντο παρὰ τῷ πρεσβυτέρῳ
(3) δειπνῆσαι μετ' αὐτοῦ, ἅμα καὶ τῶν τριῶν ἀδελφῶν αὐτῶν.
.3 (4) τὰ δὲ ἐπικείμενα ταῖς θεραπαινίσιν, ἐπειδὴ γὰρ καὶ ⟨οἱ⟩
υἱοί μου ἀνέκειντο τοῖς ἀρρενικοῖς δούλοις τοῖς διακονοῦσιν·
.4 ἀνιστάμενος οὖν ἐγὼ κατὰ ⟨τὸ⟩ πρωῒ ἀνέφερον ὑπὲρ αὐτῶν
θυσίας κατὰ τὸν ἀριθμὸν αὐτῶν περιστερὰς τριακοσίας,
.5 ἐρίφους αἰγῶν πεντήκοντα καὶ πρόβατα δώδεκα· ταῦτα πάντα
μετὰ τὴν σύνταξιν ἐκέλευον κατασκευασθῆναι ἐκ περιττοῦ καὶ
.6 ἀναλωθῆναι τοῖς πτωχοῖς· καὶ ἔλεγον αὐτοῖς ἐγώ
ταῦτα λαμβάνετε περιττὰ μετὰ τὴν σύνταξιν
ἵνα δεηθῆτε ὑπὲρ τῶν τέκνων μου·
.7 (6) μὴ ἄρα ⟨οἱ⟩ υἱοί μου ἥμαρτον ἐνώπιον κυρίου λέγοντες
μετὰ καταφρονήσεως ὅτι
(7) ἡμεῖς ἐσμὲν τέκνα τοῦ πλουσίου τούτου ἀνδρός,
ἡμῶν δὲ ἐστιν τὰ χρήματα ταῦτα·
.8 διὰ τί δὲ καὶ διακονοῦμεν;
.9 ὅτι βδέλυγμά ἐστιν ἐναντίον κυρίου ἡ ὑπερηφανία.

13.5a   curse PV: denounce (katēgorounto) S
13.5a   with contempt SV: + of the poor (see 13.4) P
13.5b   who will SPV: what will he cj Kraft
13.5b   filled SP: + and satiated V
13.6   kind SP: + to them V
14.2   arise SP: linger (?) V
14.2   and play for them (masc. = the servants of 13.4) SP: om V
14.2   and they (fem. = the widows) would chant (or "sing") SP: +
      in response V (see 31.8, 33.1, 43.1)
14.4   for them SV: om P
14.5   contempt SV: + that is, of the psalm P (but see 13.5a)
15.2   And they went SP: And along with their three sisters
      they went V (see 15.2)

```
 .5a       And they would curse me with contempt, saying,
 .5b          Who will provide for us from his meats that we might be filled?
 .6        Yet I was exceedingly kind!

14.1       And I used to have six psalms and a ten-stringed lyre.
  .2       And I would arise daily after the widows were fed and I would
           take the lyre and play for them [the servants], and they [the
           widows] would chant. And by means of the psaltery I would remind
  .3       them [the widows] of God so that they might glorify the Lord.
  .4       And if my maidservants ever began murmuring, I would take
           up the psaltery and play for them the payment of recompense.
  .5       And I would make them stop murmuring in contempt.

15.1       And after the ministry of serving [tables], my children daily
  .2       took their meal. And they went in to their older
     (3)   brother to dine with him and with their three sisters.
  .3a      And they [the sisters] were attended by the maidservants
  .3b (4)  just as my sons were also dependent on the male slaves who served
  .4       [them]. I therefore, rising early, would offer up sacrifices on
           their behalf in the following amounts: 300 doves, 50 goat's kids
  .5       and 12 sheep. Everything over and above the prescribed ritual
           portion I would order to be considered superfluous and expended
  .6a      on the indigent. And I would say to them:
  .6b         Take the things that remain after the prescribed ritual portion
  .7a (6)  so that you may pray on behalf of my children. Perhaps
           my sons have sinned before the Lord, saying with contempt:
  .7b (7)     We are sons of this rich man, and these goods
  .8              are ours. Why then do we also serve?
  .9       For pride is an abomination before the Lord.
```

```
15.2     to dine with him SP: and they would hold a drinking bout
           (or "make wine") V
15.2     and with - sisters S: also taking along with them
           the three sisters P: om V (see 15.1)
15.3     om entire verse V [see above, p.8]
15.4     in the following - doves SP: om V
15.4     12 SP: 19 V
15.5     Everything...expended S: Everything...order to be prepared P;
           I would give these superfluous things to expend V
15.6b    after - so that SP: and Vslav
15.7a    Lord SVslav: + by boasting P
15.7b    and - ours SP: give us these our goods V
15.9     For pride SP: Saying these things out of pride
           they angered God, and pride V
15.9     the Lord SV: God P
```

.10(9)   καὶ πάλιν ἐξαιρέτως μόσχον ἀνέφερον ἐπὶ τὸ θυσιαστήριον
         τοῦ θεοῦ λέγων
              μήποτε ⟨οἱ⟩ υἱοί μου κακὰ ἐνενόησαν ἐν τῇ καρδίᾳ αὐτῶν
              πρὸς τὸν θεόν.

16.1   'ἐμοῦ δὲ τοῦτο ποιοῦντος ἐν τοῖς ἑπτὰ ἔτεσιν μετὰ ⟨τὸ⟩ τὸν
  (2)   ἄγγελον ὑποδεῖξαί μοι, εἶτα μετὰ τὸ εἰληφέναι τὴν ἐξουσίαν
  (3)   τὸν Σατανᾶν, τό⟨τε⟩ λοιπὸν κατῆλθεν ἀνηλεῶς καὶ ἐφλόγισεν
         τὰς ἑπτὰ χιλιάδας τῶν προβάτων τὰ ἐκταγέντα εἰς τὴν ἔνδυσιν
         τῶν πτωχῶν καὶ τῶν χηρῶν, καὶ τὰς τρισχιλίους καμήλους καὶ
         τὰς πεντακοσίας ὀνάδας καὶ τὰ πεντακόσια ζεύγη τῶν βοῶν.
.2 (4)   ταῦτα πάντα ἀνεῖλεν δι' αὐτοῦ καθ' ἣν εἴληφεν ἐξουσίαν κατ'
.3 (5)   ἐμοῦ. καὶ τὰ λοιπὰ τῶν κτηνῶν μου ᾐχμαλωτίσθησαν ὑπὸ τῶν
  (6)   συμπολιτῶν μου τῶν παρ' ἐμοῦ εὐεργετηθέντων σφοδρῶς, νυνὶ
         δὲ ἐπανισταμένων μοι καὶ ἀφαιρουμένων τὰ ὑπόλοιπα τῶν
.4 (7)   θρεμμάτων μου. καὶ τῶν ὑπαρχόντων μοι ἀνήγγειλάν μοι τὴν
         ἀπώλειαν, καὶ ἐδόξασα τὸν θεὸν καὶ οὐκ ἐβλασφήμησα.

17.1   Τότε ὁ διάβολος ἐγνωκώς μου τὴν καρδίαν κατεμηχανήσατό
  (2)   ⟨με⟩, μετασχηματισθεὶς εἰς βασιλέα τῶν Περσῶν, καὶ ἐπέστη
         τῇ ἐμῇ πόλει, συναγαγὼν πάντας τοὺς ἐν αὐτῇ πανούργους.
.2 (3)   καὶ ἐλάλησεν αὐτοῖς μετὰ ἀπειλῆς λέγων
              οὗτος ὁ ἀνὴρ ὁ 'Ιωβάβ, ὁ ἀναλώσας πάντα τὰ ἀγαθὰ τῆς γῆς
              καὶ μηδὲν καταλειπών, ὁ διαδεδωκὼς τοῖς δεομένοις καὶ
  (4)   τοῖς τυφλοῖς καὶ χωλοῖς, καὶ τὸν μὲν ναὸν τοῦ θεοῦ κάθηλεν
.3   ἀφανίσας τὸν τόπον τῆς σπονδῆς· διὸ καὶ ἐγὼ ἀποδώσω αὐτῷ
              καθὰ ἔπραξεν μετὰ τοῦ οἴκου τοῦ μεγάλου θεοῦ.
.4   συνέλθατε οὖν καὶ σκυλεύσατε ἑαυτοῖς πάντα τὰ ζῷα καὶ ὅσα
              ἔχει ἐπὶ τῆς γῆς.

15.10a   And again - God SP (carefully offered up...around S; offered a
         select...on P): But I also offered up calves to the one at
         the altar V
15.10   saying, Possibly SV: lest P
15.10b   heart PV (= Job 1.5A): mind S (= Job 1.5 BS)
16.1   And as - finally SP: While I was living in this manner, the devil
         could not endure the good, but after he departed he demanded from
         God (to make) war on me V [on the chronology of V, see also
         21.1, 22.1, 26.1b, 27.9, and the ending]
16.1   this P(V): these things (tauta) S
16.1   and burned SP: and first burned V
16.1   7000 SP: multitude of V
16.1   appointed - widows S(P): om V
16.1   the indigent and Sslav: om P
16.1   and the 3000 SP: then the V
16.1-3   and the 500 - animals SP: then the cows and all the cattle--he
         burned some, others were confiscated, not only by enemies but also
         by those who had been treated well by me V

15.10-17.4   39

.10a (9)   And again, I carefully offered up a calf on the altar of God saying,
.10b   Possibly my sons have harbored evil thoughts in their
                  heart aginst God.

16.1   And as I was doing this during the seven years after the
     (2)   angel had made the disclosure to me, then Satan -- when he had
     (3)   received the authority -- finally came down unmercifully and
            burned up the 7000 sheep which had been appointed for the
            clothing of the indigent and the widows, and the 3000 camels,
 .2 (4)   and the 500 she-asses, and the 500 yoke of oxen. All these
            things he destroyed by himself, in accord with the authority
 .3 (5)   he had received against me. And the rest of my herds were
     (6)   confiscated by my fellow-countrymen, who had been treated
            exceptionally well by me but who now rose up against me and
 .4 (7)   took away the remainder of my animals. And they reported to me
            the destruction of my goods, and I glorified God and did not
            blaspheme.

17.1   Then the devil, having come to know my heart, laid a plot
     (2)   <against me>, by disguising himself as the king of the Persians,
            and he came against my city gathering all the opportunists in
 .2a (3)   it. And he spoke to them with a boastful promise saying:
 .2b   This man Jobab is the one who used up all the good things of the
                  earth and left nothing, who distributed to the needy and the
     (4)   blind and lame, and who tore down the temple of God, destroying
 .3   the place of the libation. Therefore, I also shall repay him
            in accord with what he did with the house of the great God.
 .4   Come along, then, and take as spoils for yourselves all his
            animals and as much as he has on earth.

16.3   exceptionally S: om P
16.4   And they - goods and SP: And the shepherds came and announced
              these things to me and when I heard V
17.1   heart SP: perseverance (karterian) V
17.1   <against me> P(V): om S
17.1   by...and SV: and...(om) P
17.1-2a   gathering - spoke SP: And gathering everyone in it, he spoke cleverly V
17.2b   Jobab SP: Job Vslav
17.2b   who distributed - lame and SP: om V
17.2b   tore down SP: destroyed and demolished V
17.2b   God SV: pr the great P (see 17.3)
17.2b   destroying...libation S: and destroyed...libation P: om V
17.3   with the SV: against the P
17.3   the great SV: om P (see 17.2)
17.4   Come - earth SP: Now then, come up with me and we shall take as
              spoils all the belongings in his house V

.5 καὶ αὐτοὶ ἀποκριθέντες εἶπον αὐτῷ
.6 ἔχει ἑπτὰ υἱοὺς καὶ θυγατέρας τρεῖς· μὴ ἄρα καταφύγωσιν
    εἰς ἑτέρας χώρας καὶ ἐντύχωσιν καθ' ἡμῶν ὡς τυραννούντων,
    καὶ λοιπὸν ἐπαναστάντες ἀποκτείνωσιν ἡμᾶς.
.7 (6) καὶ εἶπεν αὐτοῖς
.8 μὴ φωβῆσθε ὅλως· τὰ γὰρ πλείω τῶν κτηνῶν αὐτοῦ ἀπώλεσα
    ἐν πυρί, τὰ δὲ ἄλλα ᾐχμαλώτευσα, καὶ ἰδοὺ ⟨καὶ⟩ τὰ τέκνα
    ⟨αὐτοῦ⟩ ἀπολέσω.

18.1 Καὶ ταῦτα λέγων αὐτοῖς, ἀπελθὼν κατέβαλεν τὸν οἶκον ἐπὶ
.2   τὰ τέκνα μου καὶ ἀνεῖλεν αὐτά· καὶ οἱ συμπολῖται ἰδόντες
     ὅτι ἀληθῆ γέγονεν τὰ εἰρημένα ὑπ' αὐτοῦ ἐπελθόντες ἐδίωξάν
.3   με καὶ πάντα τὰ ἐν τῇ οἰκίᾳ μου διήρπαζον. οἱ ἐμοὶ
.4   ὀφθαλμοὶ τοὺς λύχνους ποιοῦντες ἔβλεπον· ἐπάνω τῶν τραπεζῶν
     μου καὶ τῶν κραββάτων μου ἄνδρες εὐτελεῖς καὶ ἄτιμοι ἦσαν,
.5 (4) καὶ οὐκ ἠδυνάμην φθέγξασθαι τὶ κατ' αὐτῶν· ἠτονημένος γὰρ
     ἤμην ὡς γυνὴ παρειμένη τὰς ὀσφύας ἀπὸ τοῦ πλήθους τῶν ὠδίνων,
   (5) μνησθεὶς μάλιστα τοῦ προσημανθέντος μοι πολέμου ὑπὸ τοῦ
     κυρίου διὰ τοῦ ἀγγέλου αὐτοῦ καὶ ⟨τῶν⟩ ἐγκωμίων τῶν
.6   λαληθέντων μοι· καὶ ἐγενόμην ὡς θέλων εἰσβαλεῖν εἰς πόλιν
     τινὰ ἰδεῖν τὸν ἑαυτῆς πλοῦτον καὶ κληρονομεῖν μέρος τῆς
   (7) δόξης αὐτῆς, καὶ ὡς ὅτε μὲν φορτίον ἐμβαλλόμενος ἐν
     θαλασσίῳ πλοίῳ καὶ μεσοπελαγίσας ἰδὼν τὴν τρικυμίαν καὶ
     τὴν ἐναντίωσιν τῶν ἀνέμων, ἔρριψεν δὲ εἰς θάλασσαν τὸ
     φορτίον λέγων
       θέλω ἀπολέσθαι τὰ πάντα μόνον εἰσελθεῖν εἰς τὴν πόλιν
       ταύτην ἵνα κληρονομήσω τὰ κρείττονα τῶν σκευῶν καὶ
       τὸ πλοῖον.
.7 (8) οὕτως κἀγὼ ἡγησάμην τὰ ἐμὰ νῦν οὐδὲν ὡς προσεγγίζειν τῇ
     πόλει περὶ ἧς λελάληκέν μοι ὁ ἄγγελος.

17.6 tyrants SP: their tyrants V
17.6 ultimately revolt SP: the rest (or "their descendants") come
      upon us with might (or "with an army") V
17.8 For - flocks S: Most of his possessions P; His flocks and
      his abundance V
17.8 I have SV: + already P (see also later in verse)
17.8 behold SV: already P (See also earlier in verse)
17.8 I shall destroy SV (see slav): om P
17.8 ⟨his⟩ children ⟨as well⟩ PV: the children S
18.2 what he had SV: what had been P
18.3 acting as lamps cj Kraft (see Sslav, above p.8): om PV

.5   And they answered and said to him:
.6   He has seven sons and three daughters. Perhaps they might flee
            to other regions and plead against us as tyrants and ultimately
            revolt and kill us.
.7   (6) And he said to them,
.8   Have no fear at all. For the majority of his flocks I have
            destroyed by fire, and the others I confiscated, and behold
            I shall destroy <his> children <as well>.

18.1   And as he said these things to them, he departed and toppled the
.2   house upon my children and destroyed them. And my countrymen, when
          they saw that what he had said actually took place, attacked and
          drove me away and began to snatch up all the things in my house.
.3-.4   My eyes, acting as lamps, searched out. Cheap and worthless men
          were at my tables and my couches, and I was unable to utter a thing
.5   (4) against them. For I was exhausted, as a woman paralyzed in her
     (5) loins by the magnitude of birth pangs, remembering most of all
          the battle foretold me by the Lord through his angel and <the>
.6a (6) encomia which had been told to me. And I became as one who wishes
          to enter a certain city to see its wealth and obtain a portion of
.6b (7) its splendor, and when he embarks with cargo in a sea-going ship
          and at mid-ocean sees the surging water and the opposition of the
          winds he throws the cargo into the sea, saying:
.6c   I am willing for everything to be lost solely to enter this
            city so that I might obtain the things more valuable than
            the discarded objects, and the ship.
.7   (8) Thus I also now considered my possessions as nothing compared
          to approaching the city about which the angel had spoken to me.

18.4   searched out S: saw that P; saw the plundering of my house and V
18.4   a thing against them SV: om P
18.5   and <the> (om S) eulogies - told to me SP: om V
18.6a-b   who wishes - splendor and SP: om V
18.6c   obtain SP: make profit from the salvaged ship and V
18.6c   and (save) the ship S: and than the ship P; om V (see
            earlier in verse)
18.7   now S[(?) the text of S is blurred at this point]: om PV
18.7   as nothing - to me SP: om V
18.7   approaching S: om P

19.1   'Ελθόντος δὲ τοῦ ἑτέρου ἀγγέλου καὶ δηλώσαντός μοι τὴν τῶν
  (2)   ἐμῶν τέκνων ἀπώλειαν, ἐταράχθην μεγάλῃ ταραχῇ καὶ διέρρηξά
        μου τὰ ἱμάτια λέγων τῷ ἀπαγγέλλοντι μοι
            πῶς οὖν σὺ ἐσώθης;
 .2 (3) καὶ τότε ἐγὼ συνιδὼν τὸ γενόμενον ἀνεβόησα λέγων
   (4)   ὁ κύριος ἔδωκεν, ὁ κύριος ἀφείλατο·
 .3   ὡς τῷ κυρίῳ ἔδοξεν, οὕτως καὶ ἐγένετο·
 .4   εἴη τὸ ὄνομα κυρίου εὐλογημένον.

20.1   Τῶν οὖν ὑπαρχόντων μοι πάντων ἀπολομένων ἔμαθεν ὁ Σατανᾶς
 .2   ὅτι οὐδὲν δύναταί <με> εἰς ὀλιγωρίαν τρέψαι· καὶ ἀπελθὼν
        ἠτήσατο τὸ σῶμά μου παρὰ τοῦ κυρίου ἵνα ἐπενέγκῃ μοι πληγήν·
 .3   καὶ τότε παρέδωκέν με ὁ κύριος εἰς χεῖρας αὐτοῦ χρή<σα>σθαι
        τῷ σώματί μου ὡς ἠβούλετο, τῆς δὲ ψυχῆς μου οὐκ ἔδωκεν αὐτῷ
 .4   ἐξουσίαν. καὶ προσῆλθεν καθημένου μου ἐπὶ τὸν θρόνον μου
 .5   καὶ πενθοῦντι τὴν τῶν τέκνων μου ἀπώλειαν· καὶ ὁμοιώθη
 .6   μεγάλῃ καταιγίδι καὶ τὸν θρόνον μου κατέστρεψεν· καὶ ἐποίησα
        ὥρας τρεῖς ὑπὸ τὸν θρόνον μου μὴ δυνάμενος ἐξελθεῖν.
 .7 (6) καὶ ἐπάταξέν με πληγὴν σκληρὰν ἀπὸ κορυφῆς ἕως ὀνύχων τῶν
 .8 (7) ποδῶν μου. καὶ ἐν μεγάλῃ ταραχῇ καὶ ἀδημονίᾳ ἐξῆλθον τὴν
    (8) πόλιν <καὶ> καθεσθεὶς ἐπὶ τῆς κοπρίας σκωληκόβρωτον εἶχον
 .9   τὸ σῶμά μου· καὶ συνέβρεχον τὴν γῆν ἐκ τῆς ὑγρασίας καὶ
 .10(9) ἰχῶρες τοῦ σώματός μου· σκώληκες πολλοὶ ἦσαν ἐν αὐτῷ καὶ
        εἴποτε ἀφήλατο σκώληξ, ἧρον αὐτὸν καὶ κατήγγιζον εἰς τὸ
        αὐτὸ λέγων
            παράμεινον ἐν τῷ αὐτῷ τόπῳ ἐν ᾧ ἐτέθης ἄχρις οὗ
            ἐπισταλῇ σοι ὑπὸ τοῦ κελεύσαντός σοι.

21.1   Καὶ ἔτη τεσσαράκοντα ὀκτὼ ἐποίησα καθεζόμενος ἐν τῇ κοπρίᾳ
   (2) ἐκτὸς τῆς πόλεως ἐν ταῖς πληγαῖς ὥστε με ἰδεῖν, τέκνα μου,

---

19.1a   And when SP: then V
19.1a   another messenger (or "angel") SV: the last messenger/angel P
19.1a   children SP: + and V
19.1b-.2a saying - saying SP: and said V
19.1b   me S: om P
20.1   When-realized SP: Therefore when Satan saw V(slav)
20.1   <me> PV: om S
20.2   And SP: om V
20.2   disease (or "plague") S P :   + because the evil one could not
          bear my endurance V
20.3   And SP: om V
20.4   the destruction of SP: om V
20.5   throne SP: + knocking me on the ground V

19.1a		And when another messenger had come and had disclosed to me
.1b	(2)	the destruction of my children, I was deeply disturbed and I tore my garments, saying to the one who brought me the report,
.1c		How then were you saved?
.2a	(3)	And then when I understood what had happened I cried aloud saying,
.2b	(4)	The Lord has given, the Lord has taken away.
.3		As the Lord decided, so has it happened.
.4		Blessed be the name of the Lord.
20.1		When therefore all my possessions were destroyed, Satan realized
.2		that nothing could induce <me> to be contemptuous. And he went and asked the Lord for my body so that he might inflict me with
.3		a disease. And then the Lord delivered me into his hands to deal with my body as he wished, but he did not give him authority
.4		over my soul. And he came to me as I was sitting on my throne
.5		and was in mourning over the destruction of my children. And he
.6		was like a great hurricane and overturned my throne. And I spent
.7	(6)	three hours under my throne unable to leave. And he struck me with a cruel disease from the top of my head to the soles of my
.8	(7)	feet. And in great confusion and distress I left the city, <and>
.9	(8)	as I sat on the dung-heap my body was infested by worms. And discharges from my body also combined to drench the ground with
.10a	(9)	their moisture. There were many worms in it and if a worm fell off, I would pick it up and return it to the same place saying:
.10b		Stay in the same place in which you were put until you receive instructions from the one who commanded you.
21.1a		And I spent forty-eight years sitting on the dung-heap outside of
.1b	(2)	the city beset by diseases so that I saw, my children, with my own

---

20.6	I spent SV: he spent P
20.6	under (on P) - leave SP: lying on floor V
20.7	the top - soles (let. "toenails") of my feet SVslav: feet to head P
20.8	<and> PV: om S
20.9	discharges - moisture SP: I wet the ground with excessive moisture and discharges flowed from my body and V
20.10a	in it SV: in my body P
20.10a	fell off S: left my body V; got on (eph- for aph-) P
20.10b	put SP: assigned V
20.10b	receive instructions from SV: are authorized by P
21.1a	48 years SP: seven years Vslav [see note at 16.1]
21.1a	sitting SV: om P
21.1b	so that SP: and Vslav
21.1b	children SP: pr lamented (or "longed for") V

ἐν τοῖς ἐμοῖς ὀφθαλμοῖς τὴν ταπεινήν μου γυναῖκα ὑδροφοροῦσαν
εἰς οἶκον τινὸς ἀσχήμονος ὡς παιδίσκην ἕως οὗ λάβῃ ἄρτον
.2 (3)   καὶ προσενέγκῃ μοι· καὶ ἐγὼ κατανενυγμένος ἔλεγον
ὢ τῆς ἀλαζονείας τῶν ἀρχόντων τῆς πόλεως ταύτης, ⟨οὓς⟩
οὐδὲ ἀξίους εἶναι κυνῶν τῶν ἐμῶν νομάδων ἡγοῦμαι·
.3   ὅτι πῶς χρῶνται τῇ γαμετῇ μου ὡς δουλίδι;
.4   καὶ μετὰ ταῦτα ἀνελάμβανον λογισμὸν ⟨μακρόθυμον⟩.

22.1   Καὶ μετὰ ἕνδεκα ἔτη καὶ αὐτὸν τὸν ἄρτον ἀφείλαντο τοῦ μὴ
προσενεχθῆναί μοι μόλις ἐπιτρέψαντες ἔχειν αὐτὴν τὴν ἰδίαν
.2   τροφήν· καὶ αὐτὴ λαμβάνουσα διεμέριζεν ἑαυτῇ τε καὶ ἐμοί
λέγουσα μετ' ὀδύνης
οὐαί μοι, τάχα οὔτε χορτάζεται ἄρτου.
.3   καὶ οὐκ ἐφείδετο ἐξελθεῖν ἐν τῇ ἀγορᾷ προσαιτῆσαι ἄρτον
παρὰ τῶν ἀρτοπρατῶν ἕως οὗ προσενέγκῃ μοι καὶ φάγω.

23.1   καὶ ὁ Σατανᾶς τοῦτο γνοὺς μετεσχηματίσθη εἰς ἀρτοπράτην·
.2   καὶ ἐγένετο κατὰ συγκυρίαν ἀπελθεῖν πρὸς αὐτὸν τὴν γυναῖκά
.3   μου αἰτῆσαι ἄρτον νομίζουσα εἶναι αὐτὸν ἄνθρωπον. καὶ
ὁ Σατανᾶς αὐτῇ ἔλεγεν
παράσχου τὸ τίμημα καὶ λάβε ὃ θέλεις.
.4   ἀποκριθεῖσα δὲ αὐτῷ λέγει·
πόθεν μοι ἀργύριον; ἢ ἀγνοεῖς τὰ συμβεβηκότα ἡμῖν ὧδε
.5   πονηρά; εἰ μὲν ἐλεεῖς ἐλέησον, εἰ δὲ μὴ σὺ ὄψει.
.6   καὶ ἀπεκρίθη πάλιν λέγων
εἰ μὴ ἄξιοι ἦτε τῶν κακῶν, οὐκ ἂν ἀπελάβετε ταῦτα·
.7   νῦν οὖν εἰ μὴ ἔχεις ἐν χερσίν ⟨σου⟩ ἀργύριον, ὑποθοῦ μοι
τὴν τρίχα τῆς κεφαλῆς σου καὶ λάβε τρεῖς ἄρτους·
.8   ἴσως δυνήσεσθε ζῆσαι ἐν τρισὶν ἡμέραις.
.9 (8)   τότε ἐν ἑαυτῇ ἔλεγεν
τί γὰρ μοι ἡ θρὶξ τῆς κεφαλῆς πρὸς τὸν πεινοῦντά μου ἄνδρα;

21.1b   humbled wife Sslav: first wife P; humbled wife who was so dainty and well guarded when I first took her as my bride [see 25.2a]-- I saw her V
21.1b   crude person (or perhaps "person shamefully" =S) SV (slav): nobleman (euschemonos) P
21.2a   stunned PV: + in my soul S (see 24.6)
21.2b   ⟨whom⟩ (om S) I consider - dogs. For SVslav [see Job 30.1]: om P
21.4   resumed--or "regained" or even "acquired"
21.4   rational ⟨composure⟩ (lit. "patient reasoning power") PV: reasoning power S
22.1   eleven years SP: a long time V (slav) [see note at 16.1]
22.2a   she would herself SP: I would (or "they would") V
22.2a   saying SP: as she said V
23.1   breadseller SVslav: merchant (praten) P
23.2   coincidence SV: chance (syntychian) P

		eyes my humbled wife carrying water into the house of a certain crude person as a maidservant until she could obtain bread and
.2a	(3)	bring it to me. And since I was stunned I said:
.2b		O the pretention of the rulers of this city <whom> I consider unworthy of even my roving dogs.
.3		For how can they use my spouse as a slave?
.4		And after these things I resumed my rational <composure>.
22.1		And after eleven years, they prevented even bread from being brought to me, barely allowing her to have her own food.
.2a		And when she received it, she would herself divide it between herself and me, saying with pain:
.2b		Woe is me! Soon he will not even get his fill of bread!
.3		And she would not hesitate to go out in the market place to beg bread from the breadsellers so that she might bring (it) to me and
23.1		I would eat. And knowing this, Satan disguised himself as a
.2		breadseller. And it happened by coincidence that my wife went to
.3a		him to beg bread, thinking he was a man. And Satan said to her:
.3b		Pay the price and take what you want.
.4a		But she said to him in reply:
.4b		Where shall I get money? Are you ignorant of the evils which
.5		have befallen us here? If you are compassionate, show mercy; but if not, you shall see --!
.6a		And he answered again saying:
.6b		If you were not deserving of the evils, you would not have
.7		received them. Now then if you have no money in <your> hand, give me as payment the hair of your head and take three loaves.
.8		Perhaps you will be able to live three days longer.
.9a	(8)	Then she said to herself:
.9b		What value to me is the hair of my head compared to my hungry husband?

23.2	went to him S: pr also P; + again V
23.2	bread PV: + from him S
23.2	a man PV: the man S
23.3b	pay SP: + me V
23.4b	Or SV: om P
23.4b	us SP: me V
23.4b	here SV: om P
23.5	compassionate SP: merciful V
23.5	you shall see: sense unclear--perhaps a threat (God will repay), or perhaps resignation (you must determine how I shall pay)
23.6a	again SV: her P
23.7	<your> PV: om S

.10(9)   καὶ οὕτως καταφρονήσασα τῆς τρίχος εἶπεν αὐτῷ
         ἀναστας κεῖρον αὐτήν.
.11(10) τότε λαβὼν ψαλίδα ἦρεν τὰς τρίχας τῆς κεφαλῆς αὐτῆς καὶ
.12(11) ἔδωκεν αὐτῇ τρεῖς ἄρτους πάντων ὁρόντων· ἡ δὲ λαβοῦσα ἦλθεν
.13   καὶ προσέφερέν μοι· καὶ ὁ Σατανᾶς ἠκολούθει αὐτῇ ἐν τῇ ὁδῷ
         περιπατῶν κεκρυμμένος καὶ πλαγιάζων αὐτῆς τὴν καρδίαν.

24.1   Καὶ ἅμα τε ἤγγισεν πρός με ἡ γυνή μου ἀνακράξασα μετὰ
         κλαυθμοῦ λέγει μοι
             Ἰὼβ Ἰὼβ, ἄχρι τίνος καθέζῃ ἐπὶ τῆς κοπρίας ἔξω τῆς πόλεως
             λογιζόμενος
                 ἔτι μικρόν
             καὶ ἐκδεχόμενος τὴν ἐλπίδα τῆς
.2   σωτηρίας σου; καὶ ἐγὼ πλανῆτις καὶ λάτρις τόπον ἐκ τόπου
.3   περιερχομένη· ἤδη γὰρ ἀπόλωλεν ἀπὸ τῆς γῆς τὸ μνημόσυνόν
             σου, ⟨οἱ⟩ υἱοί μου καὶ ⟨αἱ⟩ θυγατέρες, ἐμῆς κοιλίας
             ὠδῖνες καὶ πόνοι, οὓς εἰς τὸ κενὸν ἐκοπίασα μετὰ μόχθων·
.4 (3)   σὺ δὲ κάθῃ ἐν σαπρίᾳ σκωλήκων διανυκτερεύων αἴθριος
   (4)   κἀγὼ πάλιν ἡ παναθλία ἐργαζομένη ἡμέρας ὀδυνωμένη καὶ
         ἐν νυκτὶ ἕως ἂν εὐπορήσασα ἄρτον προσενέγκω σοι·
.5   οὐκέτι γάρ μοι δίδοται ὁ περιττὸς ἄρτος ἐκεῖνος ⟨ἐπειδὴ⟩
         μόγις καὶ τὴν ἐμὴν τροφὴν λαμβάνω καὶ διαμερίζω σοί τε
   (6)   καὶ ἐμοί, ἐννουμένη ἐν τῇ καρδίᾳ μου ὅτι οὐκ ἀρκετὸν
.6 (7)   εἶναί σε ἐν πόνοις, ἀλλὰ καὶ μὴ ἐμπίπλασθαι ἄρτου· ὥστε
   (8)   τολμῆσαι ἀναισχύντως ἐξελθεῖν εἰς τὴν ἀγοράν, κατανύγησα⟨σα⟩
         ἐν τῇ καρδίᾳ μου ὅτι οὐκ ἀρκετὸν πρ⟨οσαιτεῖν ἄρτον παρὰ
.7   τῶν ἀρτοπρατῶν. καὶ τὸν ἀρτοπρ⟨άτην εἶπε⟨ῖ⟩ν
             δός μοι ἀργύριον καὶ λήψει,
   (9)   κἀμὲ δεῖξαι αὐτῷ τὴν ἀπορίαν ἡμῶν καὶ ἀκοῦσαι παρ' αὐτοῦ
             εἰ μὴ ἔχεις, γυναῖκα, ἀργύριον, παρασχοῦ μοι τὴν τρίχα

23.10a   her hair SP: herself V
23.10b   arise and shear it (me V) SV (see 24.9): rise, take (<u>aron</u>) it P
23.11   removed SV: cut off (<u>ekeiren</u>) P (slav)
23.13   leading SV: he led P
24.1a   And SV: om P
24.1a   drew near me SVslav: drew near P
24.1b   and awaiting...your salvation PV: and I will receive...my salvation S
24.3   for already SV: wherefore (<u>dio</u>) P; For behold (<u>idou</u>) cj Kraft
24.3   your - perished SV: your memorial is destroyed P
24.3   the pangs and pains S(V): om P
24.4a   you SV: + yourself P
24.4b   by day - night SP: and suffering day and night V
24.5a   For - ⟨since⟩ (om S) SV(slav): For any longer P

.10a	(9)	And thus disdaining her hair, she said to him:
.10b		Arise and shear it.
.11	(10)	Then he took scissors and removed the hairs of her head and gave
.12	(11)	her three loaves, while all were looking on. And when she received
.13		(them) she came and brought (them) to me. And Satan followed her along the road walking stealthily and leading her heart astray.
24.1a		And as soon as my wife drew near me, she cried out in tears and said to me:
.1b		Job, Job! How long will you sit on the dungheap outside the city thinking,
		Only a little longer!,
		and awaiting the hope of your salvation?
.2		And I am a vagabond and a maidservant going around from place to
.3		place. For already your memorial has perished from the earth-- my sons and daughters, the pangs and pains of my womb,
.4a	(3)	for whom I toiled in vain, with hardships. But you sit in worm-
.4b	(4)	infested rottenness, passing the night in the open air; and I, for my part, am most wretched, laboring by day and suffering at night until I can obtain a loaf of bread to bring to you.
.5a		For that extra loaf is no longer given to me, <since> I scarcely receive my own food and I divide that between you
.5b	(6)	and me -- thinking in my heart that it is not (bad) enought that you are in pains, but you also do not get your fill of bread.
.6	(7)	So I ventured to go unashamedly to the market place, pierced
	(8)	to my heart that it did not suffice <to beg bread from the
.7a		breadseller. And when the bread>seller said,
		Give me money and you shall receive,
.7b	(9)	I also told him our straits and heard from him:
		If you have no money, woman, pay me with the hair of your

24.5b   but - bread S(P): and are famished for bread V
24.6   So SP: om V
24.6   pierced -<breadseller>cj Kraft (perhaps om "that it did not suffice"; text corrupt): pierced to my heart that there was not enough (money) to do business (prattein) S; even if pierced... (as in S) P; om V; and beg bread cj James; even if stunned to do so cj Brock; pierced to my heart that it probably would not suffice to beg bread from the breadseller cj Mancini; the phrase "(that) it did not suffice" may be an erroneous repetition from 24.5b (James suggests that "pierced to my heart" is also a misplaced doublet of 24.5b) [see also above, p.8]
24.7a   And when - said cj Kraft (similarly Mancini, James; see V): he said S; and when the merchant said to me V; om P
24.7a   receive SP: + loaves V
24.7b   pay me SV: pay P

.8   τῆς κεφαλῆς σου καὶ λάμβανε τρεῖς ἄρτους· ἴσως ζήσεσθε
          ἐν τρισὶν ἡμέραις.
.9 (10)   κἀγὼ ἐγκακήσασα εἶπον αὐτῷ
          ἀναστὰς κεῖρον ⟨με⟩ σεαυτῷ.
.10   καὶ οὕτως ἀναστὰς μετὰ ψαλίδος ἀτίμως ἔκειρέν μου τὴν
          τρίχα ἐν τῇ ἀγορᾷ παρεστῶτος τοῦ ὄχλου καὶ θαυμάζοντος.

25.1   τίς οὐκ ἐξεπλάγη λέγοντος ὅτι
          αὕτη ἐστὶν Σίτιδος ἡ γυνὴ τοῦ Ιωβ;
.2   ἥτις εἶχεν σκεπάζοντα αὐτῆς τὸ καθεστήριον βῆλα δεκατέσσαρα
          καὶ θύραν ἔνδοθεν θυρῶν
          ἕως ἂν ὅλως καταξιωθῇ τις εἰσαχθῆναι πρὸς αὐτήν--
(3)   καὶ νυνὶ δὲ καταλλάσσει τὴν τρίχα αὐτῆς ἀντὶ ἄρτων.
.3 (4)   ᾗ ἦσαν κάμηλοι γεμοσμένοι ἀγαθῶν
          ἀπεφέροντο εἰς τὰς χώρας ⟨τοῖς⟩ πτωχοῖς--
          ὅτι νῦν δίδωσιν τὴν τρίχα αὐτῆς ἀντὶ ἄρτων.
.4 (5)   ἴδε ἡ ἔχουσα ἑπτὰ τραπέζας ἀκινήτους ⟨ἐπὶ τῆς⟩ οἰκίας
          ᾗ ἤσθι⟨ον⟩ οἱ πτωχοὶ καὶ πᾶς ξένος--
          ὅτι νῦν καταπιπράσκει τὴν τρίχα ⟨αὐτῆς⟩ ἀντὶ ἄρτων.
.5 (6)   βλέπε ἥτις εἶχεν τὸν νιπτῆτα τῶν ποδῶν αὐτῆς
          χρυσοῦν καὶ ἀργυροῦν--
          νυνὶ δὲ ποσὶν βαδίζει ἐπὶ ἐδάφους
          ἀλλὰ καὶ τὴν τρίχα ⟨αὐτῆς⟩ ἀντικαταλλάσσει ἀντὶ ἄρτων.
.6 (7)   ἴδε τε ὅτι αὕτη ἐστὶν ἥτις εἶχεν τὴν ἔνδυσιν ἐκβύσσου
          ὑφασμένην σὺν χρυσῷ--
          νυνὶ δὲ φορεῖ ῥακώδη καὶ ἀντικαταλλάσσει τὴν τρίχα
          αὐτῆς ἀντὶ ἄρτων.
.7 (8)   βλέπε τὴν τοὺς κραββάτους χρυσοῦς καὶ ἀργυρέους ἔχουσαν--
          νυνὶ δὲ πιπράσκουσαν τὴν τρίχα ⟨αὐτῆς⟩ ἀντὶ ἄρτων.

24.9-.10 Rise - arisen SV: thus arising P (haplography)
24.9   ⟨me⟩ V (see 23.10): om S
24.9   for yourself S: om V
24.10   hair SP: + of my head V
25.1-.7   This ode breaks the sequence of the speech of Sitidos, which
          resumes in 25.8. Possibly the lament for Sitidos was understood
          as the way in which the crowd "marvelled" according to 24.10?
25.1   Who SP: + then V
25.1   saying S(V): om P   [Sigidos]
25.1   Sitidos cj James (see P/and 39.1, 40.6, 40.13): Sitida S; Sitis V
25.2b   But now she even SV: now she P
25.2b   loaves P (see 25.3b, .4b, .5b, .6b, .7b): a loaf SV(consistently in V)
25.3a   who had SV: whose P
25.3a   that S(P): and they V
25.3b   For SP: om V (see 25.4b)
25.3b   gives her SP: herself gives V

.8		head and take three loaves. Perhaps you will live three days longer.
.9	(10)	And I, behaving badly, said to him, Rise and shear <me> for yourself.
.10		And so when he had arisen he cut my hair with scissors disgracefully in the market place as the crowd stood by and marvelled.
25.1		Who would not express amazement, saying: Is this Sitidos, the wife of Job?
.2a		Who used to have protecting her chamber fourteen draperies and a door within doors, until a person was really considered worthy to gain entrance to her--
.2b	(3)	But now she even exchanges her hair for loaves!
.3a	(4)	Who had camels, loaded with good things, that used to carry (them) off to the proper places for the indigent--
.3b		For now she gives her hair in return for loaves!
.4a	(5)	See her who used to have seven tables reserved at her house, in which the indigent and every stranger used to eat--
.4b		For now she sells <her> hair for loaves!
.5a	(6)	Look at one who used to have a gold and silver basin for her feet--
.5b		But now goes by foot on the ground, But even <her> hair she gives in exchange for loaves!
.6a	(7)	See that this is she who used to have clothing of linen, woven with gold--
.6b		But now she bears a ragged garment, And gives her hair in exchange for loaves!
.7a	(8)	Look at her who used to have couches of gold and silver--
.7b		But now she sells <her> hair for loaves!

25.4-7	the initial imperatives have a singular subject for P throughout, for V only in 25.4a (otherwise plural), and for S throughout except possibly in 25.6a idetai (idete V; ide P)
25.4a	seven SPV: fifty slav (see 10.1,6)
25.4a	in which (sing.) SV: at which (pl.) P
25.4a	the indigent SP: every indigent person V
25.4b	For SP: om V (see 25.3b)
25.4b	<her> V: om SP (see 25.7b)
25.5b	But even - loaves SP: om V
25.5b	<her> cj Kraft: om SP (see 25.4b,7b)
25.6b	But now - And SP: And now (arti) V
25.7b	<her> V: om SP (see 25.4b)

.8 (9)   ἁπαξαπλῶς Ἰὼβ ⟨Ἰὼβ⟩ πολλῶν ὄντων τῶν εἰρημένων συντόμως
   (10)   λέγω σοι· ἐπεὶ ἡ ἀσθενεία τῆς καρδίας μου συνέτριψέν μου
.9   τὰ ὀστᾶ. ἀνάστηθι οὖν καὶ σὺ καὶ λαβὼν τοὺς ἄρτους
              χορτάσθητι, καὶ εἰπόν τι ῥῆμα πρὸς κύριον καὶ
.10   τελεύτα. καὶ ἐγὼ δὲ πάλιν ἀπαλλαγήσομαι ἀκηδίας διὰ
              πόνων τοῦ σώματός σου.

26.1   Καὶ ἐγὼ ἀπεκρίθην αὐτῇ
              ἰδοὺ ἐγὼ δέκα ἑπτὰ ἔτη ἔχω ἐν ταῖς πληγαῖς, ὑφιστάμενος
   (2)   τοὺς σκώληκας τοὺς ἐν τῷ σώματί μου, καὶ οὐκ ἐβαρύνθην
              τὴν ψυχήν μου διὰ ⟨τοὺς⟩ πόνους ὅσον διὰ τὸ ῥῆμα ὃ εἶπας
              ὅτι
              εἰπόν τι ῥῆμα πρὸς κύριον καὶ τελεύτα.
.2 (3)   ὅμως τὰ κακὰ ταῦτα ⟨ὑποφέρω καὶ⟩ ὑποφέρεις καὶ τὴν τῶν
.3   τέκνων ἡμῶν ἀπώλειαν καὶ τῶν ὑπαρχόντων ἡμῶν· βούλει μὲν
              ὡς ἡμᾶς λαλῆσαί τι πρὸς κύριον ἀπαλλοτριωθῶμεν τοῦ μεγάλου
.4   πλούτου; διὰ τί δὲ οὐκ ἐμνήσθης τῶν μεγάλων ἐκείνων ἀγαθῶν
.5   ἐν οἷς ὑπήρχομεν; εἰ οὖν τὰ ἀγαθὰ ἐδεξάμεθα ἐκ χειρὸς
.6 (5)   κυρίου, τὰ κακὰ πάλιν οὐχ ὑπομένομεν; ἀλλὰ μακροθυμήσωμεν
              ἐν παντὶ ἕως οὗ ὁ κύριος σπλαγχνισθεὶς ἐλεήσῃ ἡμᾶς.
.7 (6)   ἆρα σὺ οὐχ ὁρᾷς τὸν διάβολον ὄπισθέν σου ἑστηκότα καὶ
              ταράσσοντα τοὺς διαλογισμούς σου ὅπως καὶ ἐμὲ ἀπατήσῃ;
.8   βούλεται γὰρ ὑποδεῖξαί σε ὥσπερ μίαν τῶν ἀφρόνων γυναικῶν
              τῶν πλανησάντων τὴν τῶν ἀνδρῶν αὐτῶν ἁπλότητα.

25.8a   ⟨Job⟩ P: om SVslav
25.8a   Though SP: pr and V
25.8a   said SP: + to/by me V
25.8b   The weakness...crushes SV: In the weakness...are crushed P
25.9a   then SV: om P
25.10   again SVslav: om P
25.10   labors for (or perhaps "pains of") SV: labor for P
26.1b   seventeen SP: seven Vslav [see note at 16.1]
26.1b   have not - soul SV: my soul has not been as depressed P
26.1c   against PV (see 25.9b = Job 2.9e A): to (eis) S (see 26.3 = Job 2.9e BS)
26.2   ⟨I suffer⟩ - do cj Kraft (see V): You suffer (or "Do you suffer") these bad things similarly S; I suffer these bad things which you see as much as you do V; actually (holos) I suffer (or "Do I really suffer") these things as you do P
26.2   the destruction of our (om P) possessions SP: and we shall endure the destruction of our possessions V

.8a (9)   Job, <Job>! Though many things have been said generally,
            I say to you in brief:
.8b   The weakness of my heart crushes my bones.
.9a (10)   You, then, arise, and when you have taken the loaves, be
.9b   satisfied, and say some word against the Lord and die.
.10   Then I too shall again be free from weariness arising from
            (my) labors for your body.

26.1a   And I answered her:
.1b   Behold I have existed for seventeen years with diseases,
     (2)   submitting to the worms in my body, and have not been as
                depressed in my soul by <the> pains as by the word you spoke:
.1c   Say some word against the Lord and die.
.2   (3)   <I suffer> these bad things as much as you do --
            the destuction of our children and of our possessions.
.3   Would you have it that by our speaking something against the
.4   Lord we become alienated from the great treasure? And why
            have you not recalled the great (number) of those good things
.5   among which we used to live? If then we have received the
            good things from the hand of the Lord, shall we not in turn
.6   (5)   endure the bad things? But let us be patient in everything
.7   (6)   until the Lord in compassion shows us mercy. Do you not see
            the devil standing behind you and troubling your reasoning
.8   so that he might deceive even me? For he seeks to display
            you as one of the senseless women who deceive their husbands'
            integrity.

26.3   Would - speaking cj Kraft (text corrupt): and do you wish that
        we now speak V; (I) wishing (boulomenos) us to speak SP; Do
        you however wish (boulei mentoi) us to speak cj Brock
26.3   against PV: to S (see 26.1c)
26.3   we S: so that we P; and V [see above, p.8]
26.3   treasure (or "wealth") SP: + why have you spoken thus as one
        of the senseless women? V (see 26.8)
26.5   of the Lord PV: from (para) the Lord S
26.6   But SP: And V
26.6   in everything SV: om P
26.7   he might SP: you might V
26.8   entire verse om V (see 26.3)
26.8   deceive...integrity (lit. "cause...simplicity to wander"):
        probably refers to Sitidos challenging Job to compromise his
        principles, but could also indicate Sitidos bringing dishonor
        on Job by her actions

27.1 ἐγὼ δὲ πάλιν στραφεὶς πρὸς τὸν Σατανᾶν, ὄπισθεν ὄντα τῆς
γυναικός μου, εἶπον
ἐλθὲ ἐπὶ τὰ ἔμπροσθεν, παῦσαι κρυπτόμενος.
.2 μὴ ὁ λέων τὴν ἰσχὺν δεικνύει ἐν τῇ γαλεάγρᾳ;
μὴ τὸ πετεινὸν ἀνίπτα<ται> τυγχάνων ἐν καρτάλλῳ;
οὐχὶ ἀχρεῖ<ον> τοῦτο; λέγω
ἐξελθὼν πολέμησον μετ' ἐμοῦ;
.3 (2) τότε ἐξόπισθεν τῆς γυναικός μου ἐξῆλθεν καὶ σταθεὶς
ἔκλαυσεν λέγων
ἴδε Ἰὼβ διαφωνῶ καὶ ὑποχωρῶ σοι
ἀνθρώπου σαρκίνου ὄντι, ἐγώ εἰμι πνεῦμα·
.4 σὺ μὲν ἐν πληγῇ ὑπάρχεις, ἐγὼ δέ εἰμι ἐν ὀχλήσει μεγάλῃ.
.5 (3) ἐγενόμην ὃν τρόπον ἀθλητὴς παλαίων
.6 μετὰ ἀθλητοῦ, καὶ εἷς τὸν ἕνα κατέρρηξεν· καὶ ὁ μὲν
ἐπάνω τὸν ὑποκάτω ἐφί<μω>σεν πλήσας τὸ στόμα αὐτοῦ ἄμμου
.7 (4) καὶ πᾶν μέλος αὐτοῦ συγκλάσας ὑποκάτω αὐτοῦ ὄντος· καὶ
ἐνέγκαντος αὐτοῦ τὴν καρτερίαν καὶ μὴ διαφωνήσαντος μέγα
.8 (5) ἐφώνησεν ἀκμὴν ὁ ἐπάνω. οὕτως καὶ σύ Ἰὼβ ὑπόκατω ᾖς
καὶ ἐν πληγῇ ἀλλ' ἐνίκησας τὰ παλαιστρικά μου ἃ ἐπήγαγόν
σοι.
.9 (6) τότε καταισχυνθεὶς ὁ Σατανᾶς ἀνεχώρησεν ἀπ' ἐμοῦ ἐν τρισὶν
.10(7) ἔτεσιν. νῦν οὖν, τέκνα μου, μακροθυμήσατε καὶ ὑμεῖς ἐν
παντὶ συμβαίνοντι ὑμῖν ὅτι κρείσσων ἐστὶν πάντων ἡ μακροθυμία.

27.1a   back (or "in turn," "again") SP: om V
27.1a   who - wife SP: om V
27.1b   come SP: why do you not come to me V
27.1b   yourself SP: + wretched one V
27.2a   lion PV: he as a lion (?) S (supralinear hōs)
27.2b   Does the SP: nor yet a (mēpo) V
27.2b   while SP: om V
27.2c   Is this not useless cj Kraft: Not until (achri)
        (I say) this (?) S: om PV
27.2c   I say S: and now I say to you V; om P
27.2c   with SV: om P
27.3a   as - wept SP: he stood before me weeping and V
27.3b   of human flesh (lit. "of a fleshly man") SV: a fleshly man P
27.3b   I who SV: while I P (see 27.4 SV)
27.4   You SP: And you V
27.4   while I am (was S) SV: I am P (see 27.3b SV)

27.1a		And turning back to Satan, who was behind my wife, I said:
.1b		Come to the front, stop hiding yourself!
.2a		Does the lion show his strength in a cage?
.2b		Does the fledgling take flight while in a basket?
.2c		Is this not useless? I say,
		Come out and battle with me!
.3a	(2)	Then he came out from behind my wife and as he stood he wept saying:
.3b		See, Job, I am distraught and I yield to you
		who are of human flesh--I who am spirit.
.4		You have a disease, while I am greatly disturbed.
.5	(3)	I became like an athlete wrestling with another athlete,
		and one threw the other down.
.6		And the one above <silenced> the one underneath
		by filling his mouth with sand and mangling
		every limb of the one who was underneath him.
.7	(4)	And when the latter exhibited perseverance
		and did not become distraught,
		the one above gave a loud cry of surrender.
.8	(5)	So you, Job, were underneath and diseased,
		but you overcame my wrestling holds which I applied to you.
.9	(6)	Then Satan, ashamed, departed from me for three years.
.10	(7)	Now then, my children, you also must be patient in everything that happens to you, for patience is superior to everything.

27.5	I became SV: For you became P
27.5	wrestling SV: om P
27.6	And - one underneath SP: om V
27.6	silenced (or "muzzled") PV: spoke (? $eph\bar{e}sen$) S
27.6	limb SV: part ($meros$) P
27.6	who was SP: + here V
27.7	And when the latter SP: who V
27.7	did not become SV: became P
27.7	gave a loud cry SP: and he cried
27.7	of surrender: apparently the critical cry was "$agm\bar{e}n$" ("$akm\bar{e}n$" P)
27.8	diseased (lit. "in a plague") SP: + and in pain V
27.8	wrestling holds (or "tactics,""arts") SV: $pleutrika$ P (meaning undetermined)
27.8	to you SP: + and behold, I am yielding to you V (see 27.3b)
27.9	for three years SP: om V [see note at 16.1]
27.10	everything SP: + painful/distressing V

28.1   Ὅτε δὲ ἐπλήρωσα εἴκοσι ἔτη τυγχάνων ἐν τῇ πληγῇ,
.2 (2)   ἤκουσαν οἱ βασιλεῖς τὰ συμβεβηκότα μοι· καὶ ἀναστάντες
         ἦλθον πρός με ἕκαστος ἐκ τῆς ἰδίας χώρας ὅπως ἐπισκεψάμενοι
.3   παραμυθήσονταί με· ἡνίκα δὲ ἤγγισάν μοι ⟨μακρόθεν οὐκ
.4   ἐπεγίνωσκόν με⟩· κράξαντες δὲ ἔκλαυσαν, ῥήξαντος ἕκαστος
   (4)   τὴν ἑαυτοῦ στολήν· καὶ κατασπασάμενοι γῆν παρεκάθισάν μοι
.5   ἑπτὰ ἡμέρας καὶ ἑπτὰ νύκτας· καὶ οὐδεὶς αὐτῶν λελάληκέν μοι--
   (5)   καὶ οὐχὶ μακροθυμοῦντες μοι ἀλλ' ἐπειδὴ ᾔδεισάν με τὸν ἐν
.6   πολλῷ πλούτῳ ὄντα οὐδέποτε εἰκάσαντες. καὶ γὰρ ὅτε ἠρξάμην
         αὐτοῖς ἀναφέρειν τοὺς πολυτελεῖς λίθους, ἀπεθαύμαζον καὶ
         τύπτοντες τὰς χεῖρας ἔλεγον
             ὅταν ἡμῶν τῶν τριῶν βασιλέων τὰ χρήματα συναχθῇ εἰς ἓν
             ἐπὶ τὸ αὐτό οὐ μὴ ἀναλώσει τοὺς λίθους τοὺς ἐνδόξους
.7 (6)   τῆς βασιλείας σου. εὐγενέστερος γὰρ εἶ τῶν ἀφ' ἡλίου
         ἀνατολῶν.

.8 (7)   Ὁπηνίκα δὲ ἦλθον ἐπὶ τὴν Αὐσίτιδα ἐρωτήσαντες ἐν τῇ πόλει ὅτι
         ποῦ Ἰωβὰβ ὁ τῆς Αἰγύπτου ὅλης βασιλεύων;
.9   καὶ ἐμήνυσαν αὐτοῖς περὶ ἐμοῦ ὅτι
   (8)   ⟨κάθηται⟩ἐπὶ τῆς κοπρίας ἔξω τῆς πόλεως·
.10   ἔχει γὰρ εἴκοσι ἔτη μὴ ἀνελθὼν ἐν τῇ πόλει.
.11   καὶ πάλιν ἠρώτησαν περὶ τῶν ὑπαρχόντων μοι καὶ ἐδηλώθη
29.1   αὐτοῖς τὰ συμβεβηκότα μοι. καὶ ἀκούσαντες ἐξῆλθον τὴν
.2   πόλιν ἅμα τοῖς πολίταις· καὶ οἱ μὲν πολῖταί μου ὑπέδειξαν
   (2)   με αὐτοῖς, οἱ δὲ ἀντέτειναν λέγοντες μὴ εἶναί με τὸν Ἰωβάβ.

28.1	And - years SP: Then V
28.1	twenty SP: seven slav [see 28.10 and note at 16.1]
28.1	kings SV: + also P
28.2	And SV: om P
28.2	console...visited: or perhaps "encourage...examined" (see Job 2.11)
28.3	approached me SV: approached P
28.3	⟨from - recognize me⟩ P (see Job 2.12): om SVslav
28.4	and wept SP: in a loud voice V (see Job 2.12)
28.4	each...his own SVslav: they...their P (see Job 2.12)
28.4	threw (or "pulled") down earth (or "dust" "dirt") SVslav: sprinkled (katapasamenoi) earth P (see 29.4)
28.4	on themselves SP: on their own heads V (see 29.4)
28.5	spoke to me SP: spoke a word to me V
28.5	and this - wealthy S(P): And there were four of them in number-- Eliphas the king of the Temanites, and Bildad and Sophar and Elious--sitting discussing the matters that pertained to me V (see Job 2.11)
28.5	with me S: that they remained without speaking P
28.5	as one who S: before these evils when I P
28.5	while - comparable S: om PV
28.6a	when SP: + formerly they came to me and V

28.1		And when I had been afflicted with the disease for twenty years,
	(2)	the kings heard of the things which had happened to me.
.2		And they arose and came to me, each from his own region, so
.3		that they might console me as they visited. But when they approached me <from a distance, they did not recognize me>.
.4		And they cried out and wept as each one tore his own garment;
	(4)	and as they threw down earth on themselves they sat beside
.5		me for seven days and seven nights. And not one of them spoke
	(5)	to me -- and this was not due to their patience with me, but because they had known me as one who was very wealthy while
.6a		they were at no time comparable. For even when I would begin to offer them the precious stones, they would marvel and clapping their hands, say:
.6b		Whenever the goods of us three kings are brought together at the same place, they by no means match the
.7	(6)	glorious stones of your kingdom. For you are more noble than those from the east.
.8a	(7)	But when they came to Ausitis, they were asking in the city,
.8b		Where is Job who rules over all of Egypt?
.9a		And they reported to them about me,
.9b	(8)	<He is sitting> on the dungheap outside the city.
.10		For he has not come up into the city for twenty years.
.11		And again they asked concerning my possessions, and the things
29.1		which had befallen me were made known to them. And when they
.2		heard they went out of the city together with the citizens. And my
	(2)	citizens showed me to them, but they remonstrated, saying that
.3a		I was not Jobab. While they were still quite in doubt, Eliphaz,

---

28.6a	stones PV: + and S
28.6a	clapping their hands SP: om V
28.6b	Whenever SV: If P
28.6b	match (lit. "consume", "spend") SV: be comparable to (analogēse) P
28.6b	your kingdom SP: Jobab's kingdom V
28.7	you are SV: I was P
28.7	noble: or "generous"
28.8a	But SP: For then V
28.8a	Ausitis S (Lus-) P: + to visit/observe me V (see 28.2)
28.8b	of Egypt SP: + and all this region V
28.9b	<He is sitting> PV: om S
28.10	For...twenty years SP: Behold...seven years Vslav (see 28.1)
28.11	And again SVslav: Again P
28.11	the things SP: all the things Vslav
29.3a	While SP: pr And V
29.3a	Eliphaz V (and usually S, see 34.2 etc): Eliphas (S)P (consistently): om slav

.3 ἁπαξαπλῶς ἔτι ἀμφιβαλλόντων αὐτῶν, στραφεὶς Ἐλιφᾶζ ὁ τῶν
θεμανῶν βασιλεὺς εἶπεν
σὺ εἶ Ἰὼβ ὁ συμβασιλεὺς ἡμῶν;
.4 καὶ ἐγὼ κλαύσας κατεσπασάμην γῆν ἐπὶ τὴν κεφαλήν μου καὶ
κινήσας αὐτήν, αὐτοῖς ἐδήλωσα ὅτι
ἐγώ εἰμι.
30.1 ἰδόντες δὲ με κινοῦντα τὴν κεφαλήν μου κατέπεσαν εἰς τὴν
(2) γῆν ἐκλυθέντες, καὶ κοινηθέντων τῶν στρατευμάτων αὐτῶν
βλεπόντων τοὺς τρεῖς βασιλεῖς κατερρημένους ἐν τῇ γῇ ὡσεὶ
.2 (3) ὥρας τρεῖς ὡς νεκρούς. τότε ἀναστάντες συνελάλουν ἀλλήλοις
ὅτι
οὐ πιστεύομεν ὅτι οὗτός ἐστιν.
.3 (4) καὶ λοιπὸν ἐκάθισαν ἐν ταῖς ἑπτὰ ἡμέραις διακρίνοντες τὰ
κατ' ἐμέ, διαλογιζόμενοι τὰ κτήνη καὶ τὰ ὑπάρχοντά μοι
λέγοντες
(5) μὴ οὐκ οἴδαμεν τὰ πολλὰ ἀγαθὰ τὰ ἀποστελλόμενα ὑπ' αὐτοῦ
εἰς τὰς πόλεις καὶ εἰς τὰς κύκλῳ κώμας διαδίδοσθαι τοῖς
πτωχοῖς, παρεκτὸς καὶ τῶν ἐν τῇ οἰκίᾳ αὐτοῦ ἐρρημένων;
.4 πῶς νῦν εἰς τὴν τοιαύτην νεκρότητα ἐξέπεσεν;
31.1 Ἐγένετο δὲ μετὰ τὰς ἑπτὰ ἡμέρας οὕτως διαλογιζομένους
ἀποκριθεὶς Ἐλιοὺς εἶπεν τοῖς βασιλεῦσιν
προσεγγίσωμεν αὐτῷ καὶ ἐξετάσωμεν ἀκριβῶς εἰ ὅλως αὐτός
ἐστιν ἢ οὔ.
.2 οἱ δὲ μακρά μου ὄντες ὡς ἡμίσεως σταδίου διὰ τὴν δυσωδίαν
τοῦ σώματός μου, ἀναστάντες προσήγγισάν μοι ἔχοντες εὐωδίας
(3) ἐν ταῖς χερσὶν αὐτῶν, συνόντων αὐτοῖς τῶν στρατιωτῶν καὶ
θυμίαμα βαλλόντων μοι κυκλόθεν, ὅπως ἂν δυνηθῶσιν προσεγγίσαι
(4) μοι· καὶ ποιησάντες ἡμέρας τρεῖς χορηγοῦντες τὰ θυμιάματα,
.3 (5) πλησίον μου ἐγένοντο. καὶ ἀποκριθεὶς Ἐλιοὺς εἶπέν μοι
σὺ εἶ Ἰὼβ ὁ συμβασιλεὺς ἡμῶν;

29.3a   turned and S: turned to me and P: om V
29.3b   Are you Job (Jobab P: see 31.3b) - king SP: Come, let us draw
        near and see V (see 31.1b cop)
29.4   weeping SP: as they came I was informed (?) about them. And
        I wept profusely when I learned of their arrival and V
29.4   threw (down) S: sprinkled P (see 28.4); put V
29.4   shaking SP: sitting I shook my head and as I shook V
29.4   told (or "revealed to") them SP: revealed/declared V
30.1b   hushed at seeing S: troubled at seeing P; standing by (and) saw V
30.1b   about S: om PV
30.2b   We - that SV: om P
30.2b   he SP: Jobab Vslav

		the king of the Temanites, turned and said,
.3b		Are you Job, our fellow-king?
.4		And weeping I threw earth on my head, and shaking it I told them, I am.
30.1a		And when they saw me shaking my head, they fell to the ground
.1b	(2)	in a faint, and their troops were hushed at seeing the three kings collapsed on the ground for about three hours, as if dead.
.2a	(3)	Then they arose and began saying to one another,
.2b		We do not believe that this is he!
.3a	(4)	And then they sat for seven days reviewing my affairs, considering my herds and possessions, saying:
.3b	(5)	Have we not known the many good things sent out by him into the cities and the surrounding villages to be distributed to the poor, besides those also poured out in his house?
.4		How has he now fallen into such a deathly state?
31.1a		And after the seven days of deliberating in such a manner, Elious spoke up and said to the kings:
.1b		Let us approach him and investigate carefully to see if this is really he or not.
.2		But since they were about a half-stadion distant from me because of the stench of my body, they arose and approached me
	(3)	holding fragrant substances in their hands, while their soldiers accompanied them and fumigated the area around me with incense,
.3a	(4)	so that they would be able to approach me. And after they
	(5)	spent three days supplying the incense, they came near me and Elious spoke up and said to me:
.3b		Are you Job, our fellow-king?

30.3a	sat SP: were V
30.3b	also SV: om P
30.3b	poured out (?) SP: provided V
30.4	How SV: + then P
30.4	deathly state (or "mortal illness") SP: + and wretchedness V
31.1a	of - manner SP: om V
31.1a	Elious SPV (see 31.3a, 32.1a, 33.1, 41.1-7): Eliphas cop; (Eliphaz cj Riessler, accepted by Spittler) [see also 41.7 note]
31.1b	Let us SPV: pr Come cop (see 29.3b V)
31.1b	he P cop: so (houtos ; perhaps read houtos = 30.2b) S; Jobab Vslav (see 29.3b)
31.3a	three days SP: about three hours V
31.3a	they came near me and SV: and when they had come near me P
31.3a	Elious SPV: Eliphaz cj Kohler, Riessler, Spittler (see 31.1a)
31.3b	Job SV: Jobab P (see 29.3b, 31.1b V)

.4 σὺ εἶ ὁ τότε ἔχων τὴν μεγάλην δόξαν;
.5 σὺ εἶ ὁ ὡς ὁ ἥλιος τῆς ἡμέρας λάμπων πάσῃ τῇ γῇ;
.6 σὺ εἶ ὁ ὡς ἡ σελήνη καὶ οἱ ἀστέρες ἐν τῷ μεσονυκτίῳ
φαίνοντες;
.7 (6) καὶ τότε ἀποκριθεὶς εἶπον αὐτῷ
ἐγώ εἰμι.
.8 (7) καὶ οὕτως κλαύσας κλαυθμὸν μέγαν σὺν θρήνῳ βασιλικῷ
(8) ἀνεφώνησεν ὑποφωνούντων αὐτῷ τῶν ἄλλων βασιλέων καὶ τῶν
32.1 στρατευμάτων αὐτῶν. ἀκούσατε οὖν τοῦ κλαυθμοῦ Ἐλιοὺς
ὑποδεικνύοντος τὸν πλοῦτον τοῦ Ἰωβ τοῖς πᾶσιν
ποῦ τυγχάνει ἡ δόξα τοῦ θρόνου αὐτοῦ;
.2 σὺ εἶ ὁ τὰ ἑπτακισχίλια πρόβατα ἐκτάξας εἰς
τὴν τῶν πτωχῶν ἔνδυσιν--
ποῦ νῦν τυγχάνει ἡ δόξα τοῦ θρόνου σου;
.3 σὺ εἶ ὁ τὰς τρισχιλίους καμήλους ἐκτάξας εἰς
μεταφορὰν τῶν ἀγαθῶν τοῖς πένησιν--
ποῦ νῦν τυγχάνει ἡ δόξα τοῦ θρόνου σου;
.4 (3) σὺ εἶ ὁ τὰς χιλίους βόας ἐκτάξας εἰς ἀροτριάσμον
τῶν πενήτων--
ποῦ νῦν τυγχάνει ἡ δόξα τοῦ θρόνου σου;
.5 (4) σὺ εἶ ὁ τοὺς χρυσέους κραβάττους ἔχων,
νῦν δὲ καθήμενος ἐπὶ κοπρίας--
ποῦ νῦν τυγχάνει ἡ δόξα τοῦ θρόνου σου;
.6 (5) σὺ εἶ ὁ τὸν θρόνον ἔχων ἐκ λίθων πολυτελῶν,
νῦν δὲ ἐν σποδῷ καθήμενος--
ποῦ νῦν ⟨τυγχάνει⟩ ἡ δόξα τοῦ θρόνου σου;
.8 (7) σὺ εἶ ὁ τὰς ἱδρυμένας ἑξήκοντα τραπέζας τοῖς πτωχοῖς
στηρίξας--
ποῦ νῦν τυγχάνει ἡ δόξα τοῦ θρόνου σου;

31.4   formerly SPV: once (pote) cj Kraft
31.5   who was like...which shines (or possibly "who shines like") S:
        who was like P; who shines like V (see 18.3?)
31.7   then (om V) I answered and SV: I P
31.8   he wept   he uttered SP: they wept, their army also uttered V
31.8   while - (+ also P) made res. to him (om "to him" P) SP: om V
32.1a   Hear - all S(P): And again in response Elious said to me V
32.1a   Elious S (P)(V) (see 41.4): Eliphas/Eliphaz cj Riessler (etc.
        see 31.1a, 3a)
32.1a   to all S: to the servants (or "children," paisin) P
32.1b   only in S, as a title for the lament? The present structure of the
        lament is sometimes awkward. Probably an older form had the
        following sequence: 32.2,3,4,8; then 32.5,6,9 (corrected - see
        below), 11,10,12,(13) or something similar (32.7 differs in

.4		Are you the one who formerly had vast splendor?
.5		Are you the one who was like the sun which shines by day
.6		in all the earth? Are you the one who was like the moon and the stars that appear at midnight?
.7	(6)	And then I answered and said to him,
		I am.
.8	(7)	And thus as he wept he uttered a loud wail with a royal
	(8)	lament while the other kings and their troops made response
32.1a		to him. Hear then the wailing of Elious as he exposes the wealth of Job to all:
.1b		Where is the splendor of his throne?
.2a		Are you the one who marshalled the 7000 sheep
		for clothing the indigent?
.2b		Where now is the splendor of your throne?
.3a		Are you the one who marshalled the 3000 camels
		for transporting goods to the poor?
.3b		Where now is the splendor of your throne?
.4a	(3)	Are you the one who marshalled the thousand cattle
		for the poor to use in ploughing?
.4b		Where now is the splendor of your throne?
.5a	(4)	You are the one who had the golden couches,
.5b		but now is sitting on a dungheap!
.5c		Where now is the splendor of your throne?
.6a	(5)	You are the one who had the throne made from precious stones,
.6b		but now is sitting in ashes!
.6c		Where now is the splendor of your throne?
.8a	(7)	Are you the one who established the sixty special tables
		for the indigent?
.8b		Where now is the splendor of your throne?

---

style; 32.13 is a suitable summary approximating most closely the style of 32.2-4 + 8). Numerous corruptions appear in the witnesses.

32.2a   Are you: or "You are" (also 3a,4a,8a,13)
32.2b   now SV(slav): then (oun) P (also 3b,4b,10c,11c)
32.2b   the splendor of your throne SP: your splendor V (also 4b P, 7c P, 8b V, 9b V, 11c V, 12c PV)
32.3a-4a   camels - thousand SP: om V
32.5a   You are: or 'Are you" (also 6a,9a,10a,11a,12a)
32.6   om entire verse V
32.6b   but - ashes SP: om slav
32.6b   ashes S: the road (hodō) P
32.7   (6) om SV: For who opposed you in the midst of your children? For you were blossoming as a sprout of a fragrant fruit-tree! Where now is your splendor? P
32.8a   sixty SPV: 50 slav

.9 (8) σὺ εἶ <ὁ> τὰ θυμιατήρια τῆς ᾠδῆς ἐκ<κ>λησίας ἔχων--
        ποῦ νῦν τυγχάνει ἡ δόξα τοῦ θρόνου σου,
        ὅτι ἐν δυσωδίᾳ ὑπάρχεις;

.10(9) σὺ εἶ ὁ <τοὺς> χρυσέους λύχνους ἐπὶ τὰς ἀργυρᾶς <λυχνίας>
        ἔχων,
        νυνὶ δὲ προσδοκᾷς τὴν φαῦσιν τῆς σελήνης--
        ποῦ νῦν τυγχάνει ἡ δόξα τοῦ θρόνου σου;

.11(10) σὺ εἶ ὁ τὸ ἄλειμμα ἔχων ἐκ τοῦ λιβάνου,
        νυνὶ δὲ ἐν ἀπορίᾳ ὤν--
        ποῦ νῦν τυγχάνει ἡ δόξα τοῦ θρόνου σου;

.12(11) σὺ εἶ ὁ καταγελάσας τῶν ἀδικούντων καὶ ἁμαρτανόντων,
        νυνὶ δὲ ἐγένου χλεύη--
        ποῦ νῦν τυγχάνει ἡ δόξα τοῦ θρόνου σου;

33.1   Τοῦ δὲ 'Ελιοῦς μακρύναντος τὸν κλαυθμὸν ὑποφωνούντων αὐτῷ
  (2)   τῶν συμβασιλέων ὥστε γενέσθαι μεγάλην ταραχὴν καὶ καταπαυσάσης
        τῆς κραυγῆς εἶπον αὐτοῖς

.2   σιώπατε· καὶ νῦν ὑποδείξω ὑμῖν τὸν θρόνον μου
        καὶ τὴν δόξαν τῆς εὐπρεπείας αὐτοῦ τὴν οὖσαν ἐν
        τοῖς ἁγίοις.

.3   ἐμοῦ ὁ θρόνος ἐν τῷ ὑπερκοσμίῳ ἐστίν,
        καὶ ἡ τούτου δόξα καὶ ἡ εὐπρέπεια ἐκ δεξιῶν τοῦ <πατρός>
        ἐστιν ἐν οὐρανοῖς.

.4   ἐμοῦ ὁ θρόνος αἰώνιος ἐστίν--
  (4)   ὁ κόσμος ὅλος παρελεύσεται
        καὶ ἡ δόξα αὐτοῦ φθαρήσεται
        καὶ οἱ προσέχοντες αὐτῷ ἔσ<ον>ται ἐν τῇ καταστροφῇ αὐτοῦ.

.5   ἐμοῦ δὲ ὁ θρόνος ὑπάρχει ἐν τῇ ἁγίᾳ γῇ,
        καὶ ἡ δόξα αὐτοῦ ἐν τῷ αἰῶνί ἐστιν τῷ ἀπαραλλάκτῳ.

32.9a   song of the assembly (?) S: fragrant assembly (?)P; song, made
            of stones V [all texts appear to be corrupt]
32.9b-c   = SV: om 9b P; om 9c slav; reverse order
            of phrases cj Kraft
32.9c   for you are S: + now V; now you are P; but now is (nuni de) cj Kraft
32.10a   lamps SP: om V
32.10a   <lampstands>P: om SV
32.10b   moon's illumination SP: appearance (physin) of the light of
            the moon V
32.11   om entire verse slav
32.11b   discomfort (presumably physical) SP: decay (sapria) V
32.12b   joke S(P): + to everyone V
32.13(12)   om SVslav: Are you Job who had vast splendor? [see 31.4]
            Where now is the splendor of your throne? P

```
    .9a  (8)   You are the one who had the censers of the song of the assembly--
    .9b            Where now is the splendor of your throne?
    .9c              for you are in a stench!
    .10a (9)   You are the one who had <the> golden lamps over the silver
    .10b              <lampstands>, but now is waiting for the moon's illumination!
    .10c           Where now is the splendor of your throne?
    .11a(10)   You are the one who had the ointment from the frankincense tree,
    .11b              but now is in discomfort!
    .11c           Where now is the splendor of your throne?
    .12a(11)   You are the one who laughed at the unjust and sinners,
    .12b              but now you have become a joke!
    .12c           Where now is the splendor of your throne?

33.1         But when Elious had completed the course of the wailing during
             which his fellow-kings made response to him so that there was
        (2)  a great tumult, and after the outcry had ceased, I said to them:
    .2a         Be silent!  And now I will show you my throne
    .2b             and the splendor of its majesty which is among
                        the holy ones.
    .3a         My throne is in the supra-terrestrial realm,
    .3b             and its splendor and majesty are from the right hand
                        of <the Father> in the heavens.
    .4a         My throne is eternal--
    .4b  (4)        the whole world shall pass away and its splendor shall <fade>
                        and those who cling to it shall be (caught) in its demise.
    .5a         But my throne is in the holy land
    .5b             and its splendor is in the unchangeable world.
```

```
33.1    Elious SP: Eliphaz V (see 31.1 note)
33.1    and - ceased SP: but bringing a halt to their tumult V
33.1    I said SVslav: Job said P
33.2a   And now S: And V; Now P
33.2b   of its majesty SV: and the majesty P
33.2b   which - holy ones (or "holy things") SP: om V
33.3    occurs after 33.4 in V
33.3b   <the Father> P (see 33.9b): God S; the savior V; heavenly king slav
33.3b   in the heavens SV: om P
33.4a   My - eternal SVslav: om P
33.4b   and its splendor SV: the whole world, its splendor P
33.4b   <fade>PV: not pass away (ou parelthē) S
33.4b   in its demise SP: underneath V (+ 33.3 here)
33.5a   land SP: life V
33.5b   unchangeable (or "indistinguishable," "identical") world SV:
            world of the unchangeable one P
```

.6 οἱ μὲν ποταμοὶ ξηρανθήσονται
καὶ τὰ γαυριάματα αὐτῶν καταβαίνει εἰς τὰ βάθη τῆς ἀβύσσου.
.7 οἱ δὲ ποταμοὶ τῆς ἐμῆς ⟨γῆς⟩ ἐν ᾗ ἐστιν ὁ θρόνος μου
οὐ ξηραίνονται οὐδὲ ἀφανισθήσονται
⟨ἀλλ' ἔσονται⟩ εἰς τὸ διηνεκές.
.8 οὗτοι οἱ βασιλεῖς παρελεύσονται καὶ οἱ ἡγούμενοι παρέρχονται,
καὶ ἡ δόξα καὶ τὸ καύχημα αὐτῶν ἔσονται ὡς ἐν ἐσόπτρῳ.
.9 ἐμοῦ δὲ ἡ βασιλεία εἰς τὸν αἰῶνα αἰῶνος
καὶ ἡ δόξα καὶ ἡ εὐπρέπεια αὐτῆς ἐν τοῖς ἅρμασιν
τοῦ πατρὸς ὑπάρχει.

34.1 Καὶ ἐμοῦ ταῦτα λέγοντος πρὸς αὐτοὺς ἵνα σιωπήσωσιν
(2) ὀργισθεὶς Ἐλιφᾶζ εἶπεν τοῖς ἄλλοις φίλοις
τί χρήσιμον ὅτι οὕτως παραγεγόναμεν ⟨σὺν τοῖς στρατεύμασιν⟩
.2 (3) ὧδε ἵνα παραμυθησώμεθα αὐτὸν; καὶ ἰδοὺ οὗτος ἐγκαλεῖ
.3-4 ἡμῖν· διὸ ἀναχωρήσωμεν εἰς τὰς ἰδίας χώρας· οὗτος ἐν
ταλαιπωρίᾳ σκωλήκων κάθηται καὶ ἐν δυσωδίᾳ καὶ ἀκμὴν
ἐγείρεται καθ' ἡμῶν
βασιλεῖαι παρέρχονται καὶ οἱ ἡγούμενοι αὐτῶν,
ἡ δέ μοι, φησίν, ἔσται ἕως τοῦ αἰῶνος.
.5 ἀναστὰς δὲ ἐν μεγάλῃ ταραχῇ Ἐλιφᾶζ ἔκλινεν ἀπ' αὐτῶν ἐν
μεγάλῃ λύπῃ λέγων
.6 ἐγὼ πορεύσομαι· ἐληλύθαμεν γὰρ ἵνα παραμυθησώμεθα αὐτὸν
καὶ ἀκμὴν κατέλυσεν ἡμᾶς ἀπέναντι τῶν στρατιωτῶν ἡμῶν.

35.1 Τότε Βαλδᾶς ἐκράτησεν αὐτὸν τῆς χειρὸς λέγων
οὐχ οὕτως δεῖ λαλῆσαι ἀνθρώπῳ πενθοῦντι, οὐ μόνον ἀλλὰ
.2 καὶ ἐν πληγαῖς πολλαῖς ὄντι. ἰδοὺ ἡμεῖς ὅλως ὑγιαίνοντες
οὐκ ἰσχύσαμεν προσεγγίσαι αὐτῷ διὰ τὴν δυσωδίαν εἰ μὴ διὰ
.3 πλείονος εὐωδίας· σὺ δὲ ὅλως ἀμνημονεῖς Ἐλιφᾶζ
.4 ἁπλῶς νοσήσας ἐν ταῖς δυσὶν ἡμέραις; νῦν οὖν
.5 μακροθυμήσωμεν ἵνα γνῶμεν ἐν τίνι ἐστίν· μήτι ἄρα ἐξέστη

33.6b their heights of exultation (lit. "their arrogances") SV: the arrogance of their billows P
33.7a ⟨land⟩ PV: om S
33.7b nor – disappear SP: om V
33.7c ⟨but – remain⟩ PV: om S
33.8a These SP: om V
33.8b in SV: om Pslav
34.1a so that – silent SP: om V
34.1a Eliphaz SV: Eliphas P (consistently; see also note at 31.1a)
34.1b here SV: om P
34.1b ⟨with (in or among V) our armies⟩ PV: om S
34.2 this one SV: he (autos) P
34.4a This one S (or "thus he") V: he P
34.4a and (om V) in a stench SV: and stenches (or "foul odors") P
34.4a arouses SV: exalts P
34.4a against us SP: + saying V
34.4b rulers SV: powers of rule (hēgemoniai) P

.6a   The rivers will dry up
.6b   and their heights of exultation descend
                 to the depths of the abyss.
.7a   But the rivers of my <land>, in which is my throne,
.7b   are not drying up, nor will they disappear,
.7c   <but they shall remain> in perpetuity.
.8a   These kings will pass away and these rulers are passing away,
.8b   and their splendor and boast will be as in a mirror.
.9a   But my kingdom is forever and ever,
.9b   and its splendor and majesty are in the chariots of the Father.

34.1a   And when I was saying these things to them so that they would
    (2) be silent, Eliphaz became enraged and said to the other friends:
.1b   What has been the use of us thus having been here <with our
.2 (3) armies> so that we might console him? And behold this one
.3   indicts us! Therefore, let us depart to our own regions.
.4a   This one sits in the humiliation of worms and in a stench and
         at the critical moment arouses himself against us:
.4b   Kingdoms are passing away, as are their rulers,
             he says,
             but mine shall be forever!
.5   And Eliphaz, arising with great consternation, turned aside from
         them with deep sorrow, saying:
.6   I shall go. For we came so that we might console him, and at the
         critical moment he put us down in the presence of our troops.

35.1a   Then Baldas seized him by the hand, saying:
.1b   One ought not speak in such a way to a man who is mourning, and
.2   not only that, but also is beset by many maladies. Behold,
         although we are quite healthy we were not strong enough to
         approach him because of the foul stench, except by using many
.3   fragrant substances. And you, Eliphaz, are you completely
.4   forgetful (that) in fact you fell ill for two days? Now
         then, let us be patient in order that we may determine his condition.

34.4b   but mine S: but my kingdom Vslav; and behold for us it P
34.5   sorrow PV: consternation and S
34.6   at - moment SP: om V
35.1a   Baldas S (regularly; V elsewhere): Baldad P (regularly) V
35.1a   by the hand SV: om P
35.3   And SV: om P
35.3   are you - (that) S (P): became completely forgetful when cj Kraft
35.3   (that) in fact you S: Be (genou) frank V (?);
             how you were (egenou) when you P
35.3   you fell ill - days SP: om V
35.4   in order - determine SVslav: om P
35.4   his condition (lit. "in what state he is") SP: what his condition
             will be V

αὐτοῦ ἡ καρδία, μήτι ἄρα μιμνήσκεται ⟨αὐτοῦ⟩ τῆς
.6 (5)   εὐδαιμονίας τῆς προτέρας, καὶ ἐμάνη κατὰ ψυχήν; τίς γὰρ
.7 (6)   οὐκ ἂν ἐκπλάγη καὶ πάνυ τυγχάνων ἐν πληγαῖς; ἀλλ' ἔασόν
         με προσεγγίσαι αὐτῷ καὶ γνώσομαι ἐν τίνι ἐστίν.
36.1   τότε ἐγερθεὶς Βαλδᾶς προσήγγισεν μοι λέγων
         σὺ εἶ Ἰώβ;
.2   καὶ ἐγὼ εἶπον
         ναί.
.3 (2)   καὶ εἶπεν
         ἆρα ἐν τῷ καθεστῶτι ἐστὶν ἡ καρδία σου;
.4 (3)   κἀγὼ εἶπον ὅτι
         ⟨ἐν⟩ μὲν τοῖς γηΐνοις οὐ συνέστηκεν,
         ἐπειδὴ ἀκατάστατος ἡ γῆ καὶ οἱ κατοικοῦντες ἐν αὐτῇ·
.5   ἐν δὲ τοῖς ἐπουρανίοις συνέστηκεν ἡ καρδία μου
         διότι οὐχ ὑπάρχει ἐν οὐρανῷ ταραχή.
.6 (4)   ὑπολαβὼν δὲ Βαλδᾶς λέγει ὅτι
         μὲν γινώσκομεν τὴν γῆν ἀκατάστατον οὖσαν
         ἐπειδὴ γὰρ κατὰ καιρὸν ἀλλοιοῦται--
         ἐνίοτε εἰρηνεύει, ἔσθ' ὅτε καὶ πολεμεῖται·
.7 (5)   περὶ δὲ τοῦ οὐρανοῦ ἀκούομεν ὅτι εὐσταθεῖ.
.8   ἀλλ' εἰ ἀληθῶς ἐν τῷ καθεστῶτι τυγχάνεις ἐρωτήσω σε λόγον,
   (6)   καὶ ⟨ἐ⟩ὰν ἀποκριθῇς μοι πρὸς τὸ πρῶτον νοῦν,
         ἔχω σε ἐρωτῆσαι ἐν τῷ δευτέρῳ·
.9   καὶ ἐὰν ἀποκριθῇς μοι εὐσταθές,
         δῆλον ὅτι ἡ καρδία σου οὐκ ἐξέστη.
37.1   καὶ πάλιν εἶπεν
         ⟨ἐν⟩ τίνι σὺ ἐλπίζεις;
.2   κἀγὼ εἶπον
         ἐπὶ τῷ θεῷ τῷ ζῶντι.
.3   καὶ πάλιν εἶπέν μοι
         τίς ἀφείλατο σου τὰ ὑπάρχοντα ἢ ἐπήνεγκέν σοι τὰς πληγὰς
         ⟨τ⟩αύτας;

35.5   Perhaps - disturbed SP: om V
35.5   emotionally disturbed: lit. "his heart is agitated" (see 36.9;
        an idiom that appears several times in gk Jewish scriptures
        = be fearful, anxious)
35.5   perhaps he recalls ⟨his⟩ P(V): nor does he remember the S
        (mēti ara read as mēde ana- ?)
35.6   extremely panic stricken S(V): panic stricken and deranged P
35.6   when he encounters misfortunes (lit. "being in plagues") SP:
        Look at him--such a one in overwhelming evils and misfortunes/
        plagues/diseases V
35.7   his condition SP: (see 35.4 note; same variant in V)
36.1a   Then SP: And Vslav

.5		Perhaps he is emotionally disturbed; perhaps he recalls <his>
.6	(5)	former prosperity, and has become mentally deranged? For who would not be extremely panic stricken when he encounters
.7	(6)	misfortunes? But permit me to approach him so as to determine his condition.
36.1a		Then Baldas, when he had arisen, approached me saying:
.1b		You are Job?
.2a		And I said,
.2b		Yes.
.3a	(2)	And he said,
.3b		Is your heart in a stable condition?
.4a	(3)	And I said,
.4b		It is not involved with earthly things,
		since the earth and those who dwell in it are unstable.
.5		But my heart is involved with heavenly things
		for there is no upheaval in heaven.
.6a	(4)	And in response Baldas said,
.6b		We know the earth is unstable
		since indeed it changes from time to time--
		sometimes it is at peace, at other times it is at war.
.7	(5)	But as for heaven, we hear that it remains stable.
.8		But if you are really in a stable condition,
		I shall ask you about something,
	(6)	and if you answer me sensibly at first,
		I will question you a second time.
.9		And if you answer me calmly,
		it is clear that you are not emotionally disturbed.
37.1a		And again he said,
.1b		In whom do you place your hope?
.2a		And I said,
.2b		In the God who lives.
.3a		And again he said to me,
.3b		Who destroyed your possessions or inflicted on you these maladies?

36.1a	Baldas SV (see note to 35.1a)
36.2a	said SV: + to him P
36.4b	those who SP: pr all V
36.6b	time to time SV: + sometimes it travels a straight course and P
36.8	a stable SV: this P
36.9	that SV: + we will know that P
36.9	you - disturbed SPV (see note at 35.5)
37.1a	again SP: om V
37.1b	<In> V: On (epi) P (see 37.2b, 5b); (In) S
37.2b	lives PV: saves (sozonti) Sslav
37.3a	again SP: om V

.4   κἀγὼ εἶπον
        ὁ θεός.
.5   καὶ πάλιν ὑπολαβὼν εἶπεν
        εἰ τῷ θεῷ ἐλπίζεις, πῶς οὖν ἀδικήσει κρίνων, ἐπενεγκών
        σοι τὰς πληγὰς ταύτας ἢ ἀφελόμενός σου τὰ ὑπάρχοντα;
.6   εἰ δὲ καὶ ἀφείλατο, ἐχρῆν αὐτὸν μὴ διδόναι τι·
.7 (6) οὐδέποτε βασιλεὺς ἀτιμάζει στρατιώτην ἴδιον καλῶς αὐτῷ
.8   δωροφοροῦντα· ἢ τίς ποτὲ κα⟨τα⟩λήψ⟨ετ⟩αι τὰ βάθη τοῦ
        κυρίου καὶ τῆς σοφίας αὐτοῦ ἵνα τολμᾷ τίς προσάπτειν
.9 (7) τῷ κυρίῳ ἀδίκημα; ἀποκρίνου μοι, Ἰὼβ, πρὸς ταῦτα.
.10(8) καὶ πάλιν λέγω σοι, εἰ ἐν τῷ καθεστῶτι ὑπάρχεις,
        δίδαξόν με, εἰ ἔστιν σοι φρόνησις, διὰ τί ἥλιον μὲν
        ὁρῶμεν ἀνατέλλοντα ἐπὶ ἀνατολὰς, δύνοντα δὲ ἐν τῇ δύσει,
        καὶ πάλιν ἀνιστάμενοι κατὰ πρωὶ εὑρίσκομεν τὸν αὐτὸν
.11   ἐν ἀνατολαῖς ἀνατέλλοντα; νουθέτησον πρὸς ταῦτα.
.12   καὶ εἶπον
        νουθέτησόν με πρὸς ταῦτα, εἰ ἔστιν σοι φρόνησις·
38.1   ⟨ἔστιν μὲν φρόνησις⟩ ἐν ἐμοί καὶ σύνεσις τῇ καρδίᾳ μου,
        διὰ τί οὖν μὴ λαλήσω τὰ μεγαλεῖα τοῦ κυρίου;
.2   εἰ ὅλως ἂν π⟨τ⟩αίσῃ μου τὸ στόμα εἰς τὸν δεσπότην; μὴ
.3 (2) γένοιτο· τίνες γὰρ ἐσμὲν πολυπραγμονοῦντες τῶν ἐπουρανίων
        σάρκινοι ὄντες καὶ ἔχοντες τὴν μερίδα ἐν γῇ καὶ σποδῷ;
.4 (3) ἵνα οὖν γνῶτε ὅτι συνέστηκεν ἡ καρδία μου, ἀκούσατε ὃ
        ἐπερωτῶ ὑμᾶς. διὰ τοῦ στόματος ἡ τροφὴ, καὶ πάλιν τὸ
        ὕδωρ διὰ τοῦ στόματος πίνεται ἐν τῇ αὐτῇ
.5   φάρυγγι· ὅταν δὲ καταβῇ τὰ δύο εἰς τὸν ἀφεδρῶνα, τότε
.6   ἀφορίζεται ἀπ' ἀλλήλων. τίς οὖν ταῦτα χωρίζει;

37.5a   again he replied and said S: he said V; + to me P
37.5b   If...in SVslav: (om)...on (epi) P (see 37.1b, 2b)
37.5b   then SP: om V; not (ouk) cj James
37.5b   does he act unjustly cj Kraft (= Job 8.3; SV adikēsai infin.):
        can he be unjust (adikos ē) P; Brock and Spittler refer the phrase
        to Job as subject--"how is it that you consider God to be
        unjust"; James emends "how was he not unjust" (ouk adikos ēn)
37.5b   maladies (lit."plagues") SP: + and misfortunes V
37.6   If he also S: pr But V; If he gave and P
37.6   **give anything SV: have given anything at all P**
37.8-10 Kohler and Philonenko prefix the words "⟨And I said⟩" to 37.8
        (Philonenko also attaches 37.9 to the end of 37.7) and insert a
        similar formula before 37.10 ("And Baldas said" cj Kohler;
        "And again he said to me" cj Philonenko). A response by Job
        seems called for in this section. We might transfer 37.8
        after 38.8, where it fits rather well, and supply before 37.10
        "And I said"; then before 37.11 supply "And he said" (followed
        by the P text). This would help the flow of discussion consider-
        ably--note that it is Job who asks about "earthly" things in
        38.4 (compare 37.10); indeed 37.10 would make even better
        sense in the later section.

.4a		And I said,
.4b		God.
.5a		And again he replied and said:
.5b		If you place your hope in God, how then does he act unjustly when he judges, inflicting on you these maladies
.6		or taking away your possessions? If he also took it away, it would have been better for him not to give anything.
.7		A king never punishes his own soldier who serves him well.
.8		Or who can ever comprehend the deep things of the Lord and his wisdom so that someone dares to ascribe to the Lord an injustice?
.9	(7)	Answer me, Job, concerning these matters.
.10	(8)	And again I say to you, if you are in a stable condition, instruct me—if you have your wits about you, why do we see the sun rising in the east and setting in the west, and again when we get up early we find the same sun rising
.11		in the east? Advise <me> concerning these matters.
.12a		And I said:
.12b(1)		Advise me concerning these matters, if you have your wits
38.1		about you! <But I have my wits> about me, and there is understanding in my heart; why then should I not talk about the great things of the Lord?
.2		Should my mouth completely blunder respecting the master?—
.3	(2)	may it never be! For who are we to be busying ourselves with heavenly matters, seeing that we are fleshly and have
.4a	(3)	our lot in dust and ashes? Therefore, in order that you may know that my heart is composed, listen to what I ask you:
.4b		Food through the mouth, and then water through the mouth
.5		is swallowed in the same throat. But when the two fall into the latrine, they are then separated from each other.
.6		Who then divides them?

37.8	comprehend (lit. "lay hold of"; thus also "seize," "repress") PV: hide (kalypsei) S; perhaps read kataleipsetai = forsake cj Kraft
37.8	so that someone S: so that he V: or who (tis) P
37.10	instruct me SV: tell (me) (deixon) P
37.11	<me> PV: om S (but see 37.12bS)
37.11	matters SVslav: + if you are the servant (therapōn)of God P
37.12a	said S(V): + concerning these matters P
37.12b	Advise - matters S: om P (see previous note) V
37.12b	if - you cj Kraft: pr And I said S; om PV
38.1	<But I have my wits> P: om SV
38.1	and there - heart SP: om V
38.2	Should S(V): Or should P
38.2	blunder PV: fail (pese) S
38.3	and have SV: having P
38.4b	Food SV: + enters P
38.4b	mouth is swallowed (lit. "drunk") S: same mouth is drunk and sent along P; + together they go down V
38.6	Who SPV: What (ti) cj Kraft

.7 (4) εἶπεν δὲ ὁ Βαλδᾶς
         ἀγνοῶ.

.8 (5) ἐγὼ δὲ πάλιν ὑπολαβὼν εἶπον αὐτῷ
         εἰ σὺ τὴν τοῦ σώματος πορείαν οὐ καταλαμβάνεις,
         πῶς τὰ ἐπουράνια καταλάβῃ;

.9 (6) Ὑπολαβὼν δὲ καὶ Σοφὰρ εἶπεν
         οὐχὶ τὰ ὑπὲρ ἡμᾶς ἐρευνῶμεν, ἀλλὰ βουλόμεθα γνῶναι ἐὰν
.10   ἐν τῷ σαυτοῦ καθεστῶτι ὑπάρχεις· καὶ ἰδοὺ ἀληθῶς ἔγνωμεν
.11(7)   ὅτι ἡ σύνεσίς σου οὐκ ἠλλοίωται. τί οὖν βούλει ἡμᾶς ἐν
.12   σοι διαπράξασθαι; ἰδοὺ γὰρ παρόντες μεθ' ἡμῶν αὐτῶν
         τοὺς ἰατροὺς τῶν τριῶν βασιλειῶν ἡμῶν ἡγάγομεν, καὶ εἰ
         βούλει θεραπευθῆναι παρ' αὐτῶν ἴσως.

.13(8) ἀποκριθεὶς δὲ ἐγὼ εἶπον
         ἡ ἐμὴ ἴασις καὶ θεραπεία παρὰ κυρίου ἐστίν
         τοῦ καὶ τοὺς ἰατροὺς κτίσαντος.

39.1   Καὶ ἐμοῦ ταῦτα πρὸς αὐτοὺς λέγοντος, <ἦλθεν> ἡ γυνή μου
   (2)   Σίτιδος ἐν ἱματίοις ῥακκώδαις, ἀποδράσασα ἐκ τῆς τοῦ
         οἰκοδεσπότου δουλείας ᾧ ἐδούλευεν ἐπεὶ ἐκωλύετο ἐξελθεῖν
         ἵνα μὴ ἰδόντες αὐτὴν οἱ συμβασιλεῖς ἁρπάσωσιν αὐτήν·

.2 (3) ὅτε δὲ ἦλθεν, ἔρριψεν ἑαυτὴν παρὰ τοὺς πόδας αὐτῶν κλέουσα
         καὶ λέγουσα
   (4)   μνήσθητι, Ἐλιφᾶζ καὶ οἱ δύο φίλοι σου, ὅτι ὁποία τις
.3 (5)   ἤμην μεθ' ὑμῶν καὶ πῶς ἐστολιζόμην; νῦνι δὲ ὁρᾶτε τὴν
         προέλευσίν μου ἢ τί ἐνδύομαι.

.4 (6) τότε κλαύσαντες κλαυθμὸν μέγαν καὶ γενόμενοι ἐν διπλῇ
   (7)   ἀκηδίᾳ ἐσιώπησαν ὥστε τὸν Ἐλιφᾶζ ἄραντα τὴν πορφυρ<ίδ>α
.5 (8) αὐτοῦ περιρῆξαι καὶ περιβαλεῖν τὴν γυναῖκά μου. ἡ δὲ ἐδέετο
         αὐτῶν λέγουσα
         παρακαλῶ κελεύσατε τοῖς στρατιώταις ὑμῶν ἵνα σκάψωσιν

38.7a	Baldad P (see note at 35.1)
38.8a	And again S: And V: Again P
38.8b	If SV: + then P
38.8b	function (lit. "course") PV: providential foresight (pronoian) S
38.8b	the body SP: your body V
38.9a	also SP: om V
38.9b	beyond us (see SP), or possibly "concerning us" (see V)
38.9b	within yourself V: the same (stable condition)S: om P
38.12	since - traveling SV: we are traveling P; we have brought along cj James, Brock (parēgagomen--see following note)
38.12	we have brought SVslav: om P
38.12	kingdoms SP: kings V
38.12	if you SV: do you P
38.12	in - manner S: om V: + you will rest P
38.13b	treatment SV: pr my P

.7a	(4)	And Baldas said,
.7b		I do not know.
.8a	(5)	And again I replied and said to him:
.8b		If you do not understand the function of the body, how will you understand the heavenly matters?
.9a	(6)	And Sophar also responded and said
.9b		We are not investigating the things beyond us, but wish to know if you are in a stable condition within yourself.
.10		And behold, we know for a fact that your understanding has not
.11	(7)	become confused. What then do you want us to do with you?
.12		For behold, since we are traveling we have brought with us the physicians of our own three kingdoms, and if you wish you may be treated by them in the same manner.
.13a	(8)	But I answered and said:
.13b		My healing and treatment are from the Lord, who created even the physicians.
39.1		And while I was saying these things to them, my wife Sitidos
	(2)	<came> in tattered garments, fleeing from the servitude to the steward whom she served, since he had forbidden (her) to leave
.2a	(3)	lest the fellow-kings see her and seize her. But when she came she threw herself at their feet, calling and saying:
.2b	(4)	Do you remember, Eliphaz, you and your two friends, what
.3	(5)	sort of person I used to be among you and how I used to be outfitted? But now do you see how I come forth or what I wear!
.4	(6)	Then, when they had made great wailing and became doubly weary,
	(7)	they fell silent so that Eliphaz seized his purple robe to tear
.5a	(8)	if off, and threw it about my wife. But she began to beseech them saying:
.5b		I urge (that) you command your soldiers to dig through the ruins of the house that fell on my children so that

---

39.1	Sitidos P (consistently): Sitida S (here and 25.1); Sitis V (consistently)
39.1	<came> P: behold (edou) V: om S
39.1	see her SV: see P
39.2a	But SV: Then P
39.2a	calling SVslav: crying (klaiousa) P
39.2b	remember SV: + me P
39.2b	your two SP: the V
39.3	or SP: om V
39.4	when they SP: when the kings Vslav (see 39.10a)
39.4	so that Eliphaz SV: as (hos) Eliphas P (see 29.3 note)
39.4	and threw - wife SP: to clothe her V
39.5a	them SP: him V
39.5b	urge (that) SP: urge you my Lords that V
39.5b	the house SP: our house V

	τὴν πτῶσιν τῆς οἰκίας τῆς ⟨ἐπι⟩πεσούσης τοῖς τέκνοις μου
(9)	ἵνα ⟨καὶ⟩ τὰ ὀστᾶ αὐτῶν ἀσφαλισθῇ ἐπὶ μνήμης ἐπεὶ ἡμεῖς
.6	οὐκ ἰσχύσαμεν διὰ τὰ ἀναλώματα· ὅπως θεάσωμεν κἄν τὰ ὀστᾶ
.7 (10)	αὐτῶν. μὴ ἄρα ἐγὼ ἡ κτηνώδης γαστέρα θηρίου ἔχω ὅτι
	τὰ τέκνα μου δέκα ὄντα τέθνηκαν καὶ οὐδένα αὐτῶν κεκήδευκα;
.8 (11)	καὶ οἱ μὲν ἀπῆλθον εἰς τὸ σκάπτειν, ἐγὼ δὲ ἐκώλυσα λέγων
.9 (12)	μὴ κάμετε εἰκῇ. οὐ γὰρ εὑρήσετε τὰ παιδία μου, ἐπειδὴ
	ἀνελήφθησαν εἰς τοὺς οὐρανοὺς ὑπὸ τοῦ δημιουργοῦ αὐτῶν
	τοῦ βασιλέως.
.10(13)	τότε πάλιν ἀποκριθέντες εἶπον μοι
	τίς πάλιν οὐκ ἐρεῖ ὅτι ἐξέστης καὶ μαίνει εἰπὼν ὅτι
	ἀνελήφθη τὰ τέκνα μου εἰς τὸν οὐρανόν;
.11	διὸ ἔκφανον ἡμῖν τὸ ἀληθές.
40.1	ἐγὼ ⟨δὲ⟩ ὑπολαβὼν εἶπον αὐτοῖς
	ἐπεγείρατέ με ἵνα στῶ.
.2	οἱ δὲ ἐγείραντές με ἑκατέρωθεν τοὺς βραχίονάς μου
.3 (2)	ὑποστηρίζοντες· καὶ τότε σταθεὶς ἐξωμολογησάμην πρῶτον
.4 (3)	τῷ κυρίῳ· καὶ μετὰ τὴν μεγάλην εὐχὴν εἶπον αὐτοῖς
	ἀναβλέψατε τοῖς ὀφθαλμοῖς ὑμῶν πρὸς ἀνατολάς.
.5	καὶ ἀναβλέψαντες εἶδον τὰ τέκνα μου ἐστεφανωμένα παρὰ
	τῆς δόξης ἐπουρανίου.
.6 (4)	ἰδοῦσα δὲ ⟨ταῦτα⟩ Σίτιδος ἡ γυνή μου κατέπεσεν εἰς τὴν γῆν
	προσκυνοῦσα καὶ εἶπεν
	νῦν ἔγνων ὅτι ὑπάρχει μοι μνημόσυνον παρὰ κυρίου·
.7	ἀναστήσομαι δὲ καὶ εἰσελεύσομαι εἰς τὴν πόλιν καὶ καμμύσω
	ὀλίγον ⟨καὶ ἀνακτήσομαι πρὸ τῆς ὑπουργείας τῆς δουλείας μου.⟩
.8 (5)	καὶ ἀπελθοῦσα εἰς τὴν πόλιν περὶ τῶν βοῶν αὐτῆς τῶν
(6)	ἁρπασθέντων ὑπὸ τῶν ἀρχόντων ἐν οἷς ἐδούλευεν ἐκοιμήθη περὶ
.9 (7)	τὴν φάτνην αὐτῶν κἀκεῖ τετελεύτηκεν ἀθυμήσασα. καὶ ὁ μὲν

39.5b	⟨at least⟩ PV: om S
39.5b	since - unable SVslav: We were able P
39.7	like - animal V (see S): a womb like cattle or of a wild animal (?) P
39.7	died SP: + in one day Vslav
39.8a	And - dig SP: And the kings commanded that the house be dug V
39.8a	it SP: them V
39.8b	in vain PV: here (ekei) S
39.9	you - children SP: my children are not to be found V
39.9	were - heavens SP: are kept (or "guarded," "preserved") V
39.9	their king (or "of their king") SP: and king V
39.10a	Then again they SP: And the kings V(slav)
39.10b-c	when (om P) - heaven SP: because when we wish to bring up the bones of your children you forbid us saying that they have been taken up and are kept by their creator V (see 39.9)
40.1a	⟨And⟩ PV: om S
40.1a	in response SP: om V
40.3	then SP: om V

	(9)	<at least> their bones might be preserved as a memorial since
.6		we were unable (to do so) because of the costs. Thus we can
.7	(10)	look at something, even if it is their bones. Have I, like cattle, the womb of a wild animal, because my children—ten of them!—have died and I have not attended to the burial of a single one of them?
.8a	(11)	And they went off to dig, but I forbid it saying:
.8b		Don't labor in vain.
.9	(12)	For you will not find my children, since they were taken up into the heavens by the creator, their king.
.10a	(13)	Then again they answered and said to me:
.10b		Who then will not say that you are mad and raving when you say,
.10c		My children have been taken up into heaven!
.11		Now tell us the truth!
40.1a		<And> I said to them in response,
.1b		Lift me up so that I may stand.
.2		And they lifted me, supporting my arms on each side.
.3	(2)	And then having stood up I first gave thanks to the Lord.
.4a	(3)	And after the great prayer I said to them:
.4b		Look up with your eyes to the east.
.5		And when they looked up they saw my children crowned alongside
.6a	(4)	the splendor of the heavenly one. And when she saw these things, my wife Sitidos fell to the ground worshipping and said:
.6b		Now I know that I have a memorial with the Lord.
.7		And I shall arise and reenter the city and doze a little <and refresh myself prior to the duties of my servitude>.
.8	(5)	And going away into the city on account of her cattle, which had
	(6)	been seized by the rulers among whom she served, she fell asleep
.9	(7)	near their manger, and there she died, without malice. And when

---

40.3   first...to the Lord cj Kraft: + and God S; to the Lord and God slav; first...to God V; to the Father P (see 47.11 note)
40.4a   great Sslav: om PV
40.5   And - saw SVslav: and see P
40.5   one SP: king V
40.6a   these things V: then (tote) P: om S
40.6a   worshipping SP: + God V̄
40.7   om entire verse V
40.7   <and refresh - servitude> P: om S
40.8   And - rulers S(P): And after she said these things, when evening had fallen (see 40.9), she went into the city to her masters (lit. "lords") V
40.8   on account of (or "near") S: she entered the fold of P
40.8   served S: + and PV
40.8   their manger S: the manger of the cattle V; a certain manger P
40.8   and there (or kakē = "in a base condition") SV: om P
40.8   without malice (or "despondent"; perhaps "exhausted") SV: content (or "cheerfully" = euthymēsasa) P; om slav

           δεσποτικὸς ἄρχων αὐτῆς ἐπιζητήσας αὐτὴν καὶ μὴ εὑρὼν
(8)   εἰσῆλθεν ἑσπέρας οὔσης εἰς τὴν ἔπαυλιν τῶν κτηνῶν καὶ εὗρεν
.10(9)   αὐτὴν νεκρὰν ἡπλωμένην· καὶ πάντες ἰδόντες αὐτὴν ἀνέκραξαν
           μετὰ μυκήματος καὶ κλαυθμοῦ ἐπ' αὐτὴν ⟨καὶ ἡ φωνὴ διεδώθη
.11(10)   διὰ πάσης τῆς πόλεως. καὶ τότε εἰσεπήδησαν γνῶναι τὸ γεγονός
(11)   καὶ εὗρον αὐτὴν νεκράν⟩ τὰ δὲ περιεστῶτα ζῷα κλαίοντα ἐπ'
.12   αὐτήν. καὶ οὕτως προκομίσαντες ἐκήδευσαν αὐτὴν θάψαντες ἐπὶ
           τὴν οἰκίαν τὴν συμπεπτωκυῖαν ἐπὶ τὰ τέκνα αὐτῆς·
.13   ⟨καὶ⟩ κοπετὸν μέγα⟨ν⟩ ἐποίησαν οἱ πτωχοὶ τῆς πόλεως λέγοντες
           ἴδετε ⟨ἡ⟩ Σίτιδός ἐστιν αὕτη ἡ τοῦ καυχήματος καὶ τῆς
           δόξης γυνὴ ὅτι οὐ κατηξιώθη ταφῆς ἀναγκαίας.
.14   τὸν μὲν οὖν θρῆνον τὸν ὑπ' αὐτῶν γενόμενον εὑρήσετε ἐν
           τοῖς παραλειπομένοις.

41.1   Ἐλιφᾶζ δὲ καὶ οἱ λοιποὶ ⟨μετ' αὐτοῦ⟩ παρεκάθισάν μοι
(2)   ἀνταποκρινόμενοι καὶ μεγαλορημονοῦντες κατ' ἐμοῦ, ὡς μετὰ
           εἴκοσι ἑπτὰ ἡμέρας ἀναστῆναι αὐτοὺς καὶ πορευθῆναι εἰς τὴν
(3)   ἑαυτῶν χώραν, καὶ ὁρκωθῆναι αὐτοὺς ὑπὸ Ἐλιοὺς λέγοντος
.2   μείνατε ἕως καὶ περὶ τούτου δείξω αὐτῷ· ὅτι τοσαύτας
           ἡμέρας ἐποιήσατε ἀνεχόμενοι τῷ Ἰὼβ καυχωμένου εἶναι
.3 (4)   δίκαιον· ἐγὼ γὰρ οὐκ ἀνέξομαι·
.4   ἀρχῆθεν γὰρ κλαυθμὸν διετέλεσα αὐτῷ ἀναμιμνησκόμενος
.5   τῆς εὐδαιμονίας αὐτοῦ τῆς προτέρας. καὶ ἰδοὺ μεγάλως καὶ
           ὑπερβαλλόντως ἐλάλησεν λέγων ἔχειν τὸν ἑαυτοῦ θρόνον ἐν
.6 (5)   οὐρανοῖς. τοινῦν ἐμοῦ ἀκούσατε καὶ γνωρίσω ὑμῖν τὴν
           μερίδα αὐτοῦ οὐχ ὑπάρχουσαν.

40.9   when it was evening SP: om V (see 40.8)
40.9   dead SP: + on the manger V
40.10-12 the preserved texts seem to be corrupt and confused to some degree.
          Possibly the "all who saw her (om "her" P)" of 40.10 are cattle,
          who bellow and weep and perhaps even bury her in solemn
          procession (40.12 ?) [similarly James, p. c]
40.10   entire verse placed after 40.11 in V
40.10   bellowing and (see S mēkytatos kai) cj Kraft: a bellowing of P; om V
40.10   over her SP: om V
40.10-11 ⟨and the - dead⟩ P: ⟨and the - city⟩ V: om S
40.11   while - her PV: written twice in S
40.12   over (or "on," "at") SV: near (peri) P
40.13a   ⟨And⟩ PV: om S
40.13a   saying SP: + about her V
40.13b   Can this be (or "This is")--perhaps emend ē to ei cj Brock
40.13b   the woman SP: was she not a woman V
40.13b   for SP: and V
40.14   by them cj Kraft (see V = "by him"): by her S; for (ep) her P
40.14   "Paraleipomena" (lit. "things omitted," "left-overs"; thus "miscel-
          lanies" of Eliphaz? see 41.7)--the relation of this reference to
          a collection and the lament in 25.1-7 is not clear. Possibly
          25.1-7 applies an older lament for Sitidos to the specific episode

	(8)	her tyrannical ruler sought her and could not find her, he went when it was evening to the fold of the herds and found her
.10	(9)	sprawled out dead. And all who saw her cried out with bellowing and wailing over her, <and the sound was spread through the
.11	(10)	entire city. And then they rushed in to know what had happened
	(11)	and found her dead,> while the animals stood about weeping over
.12		her. And thus bringing her forth, they attended to her by burying her over the house that had collapsed on her children.
.13a		<And> the poor of the city made a great commotion saying:
.13b		Look! Can this be Sitidos, the woman of pride and splendor, for she was not considered worthy of a proper burial!
.14		So then you will find the lament made by them (recorded) in the "Paraleipomena."
41.1a		Now Eliphaz and the others <with him> sat beside me arguing and
	(2)	delivering a tirade against me, so that after twenty seven days
	(3)	they were about to arise and go to their own countries, when Elious bound them by an oath, saying:
.1b		Stay until I clarify this situation for him.
.2		For you spent so many days putting up with Job boasting that
.3	(4)	he is righteous. But I will not put up with him.
.4		For from the start I continued to make lament for him,
.5		remembering his former prosperity. And behold he has spoken grandiosely and excessively, saying that his own throne is
.6	(5)	in the heavens. Therefore, listen to me and I will make known to you his non-existent portion!

---

	of her hair being sold--a lament that also had been referred to the event of her death.
41.1a	<with him> V (+ who were amazed at these things): after these things P (see V); om S
41.1a	delivering a tirade: or "boasting"
41.1a	so that - saying SP: for 27 days saying that I had suffered these things justly, because of many sins, and that no hope remained for me. But I opposed them vehemently. And filled with wrath they arose to depart in anger. And then Elious made them take an oath V
41.1b	Stay S: + for a little V; + with me P
41.1b	I clarify SP: he might clarify V
41.1b	him SP: them V
41.4	remembering PV: while he remembered (?) S
41.4	prosperity (see 35,5) SV: + and suddenly he has elevated himself to the same height P
41.6	his non-existent SP: wherein is his V

.7 τότε Ἐλιοὺς ἐμπλησθεὶς ἐν τῷ Σατανᾷ ἐξεῖπέν μοι λόγους
(6) θρασεῖς οἵτινες ἀναγεγραμμένοι εἰσιν ἐν τοῖς παραλειπομένοις
τοῦ Ἐλιφᾶζ.

42.1 Μετὰ δὲ τὸ παύσασθαι αὐτὸν ἀναφανεῖς μοι ὁ κύριος διὰ
(2) λαίλαπος καὶ νεφῶν εἶπεν μεμφόμενος τὸν Ἐλιοὺς καὶ
ὑποδείξας μοι τὸν ἐν αὐτῷ λαλήσαντα μὴ εἶναι ἄνθρωπον ἀλλὰ
.2 (3) θηρίον. τοῦ δὲ κυρίου λαλήσαντός μοι διὰ τῆς νεφέλης
ἤκουον τῆς φωνῆς τοῦ λαλοῦντός μοι.
.3 (4) καὶ μετὰ τὸ παύσασθαι τὸν κύριον λαλοῦντά μοι εἶπεν ὁ κύριος
τῷ Ἐλιφᾶζ
(5) ἥμαρτες σὺ καὶ οἱ δύο σου φίλοι·
.4 οὐ γὰρ ἐλαλήσατε ἀληθὲς κατὰ τοῦ θεράποντός μου Ἰώβ·
.5 (6) διὸ ἀναστάντες ποιήσατε αὐτὸν ὑπὲρ ὑμῶν ἀναφέρειν θυσίας
.6 ὅπως ἀφεθῇ ὑμῶν ἡ ἁμαρτία· εἰ μὴ γὰρ δι' αὐτόν ἀπώλεσα
ἂν ὑμᾶς.
.7 καὶ αὐτοὶ δὲ προσήνεγκάν μοι τὰ πρὸς θυσίαν·
.8 καὶ ἐγὼ λαβὼν ἀνήνεγκα ὑπὲρ αὐτῶν καὶ ὁ κύριος προσδεξάμενος
ἀφῆκεν αὐτοῖς τὴν ἁμαρτίαν.

43.1 Τότε Ἐλιφᾶζ καὶ Βαλδᾶς καὶ Σοφὰρ γνόντες ὅτι ἐχαρίσατο
αὐτοῖς ὁ κύριος τὴν ἁμαρτίαν αὐτῶν, τὸν δὲ Ἐλιοὺς οὐ
(2-3) κατηξίωσεν, ἀναλαβὼν Ἐλιφᾶζ εἶπεν ὕμνον, ἐπιφωνούντων
⟨αὐτῷ⟩ τῶν ἄλλων φίλων καὶ τῶν στρατευμάτων πλησίον τοῦ
.2 (4) θυσιαστηρίου· ἔλεγεν οὕτως Ἐλιφᾶζ
περιῆρται ἡμῶν ἡ ἁμαρτία καὶ ἀπέστη ἡμῶν ἡ ἀνομία·
(5) Ἐλιοὺς ὁ μόνος πονηρὸς μνημόσυνον οὐχ ἕξει ἐν τοῖς ζῶσιν.
.3 καὶ ὁ λύχνος αὐτοῦ σβεσθεὶς ἠφάνισεν τὸ φέγγος αὐτοῦ
(6) ἡ δὲ τῆς λαμπάδος αὐτοῦ δόξα ἀποβήσεται αὐτῷ εἰς κρίμα·
.4 ὅτι οὗτός ἐστιν ⟨ὁ⟩ τοῦ σκότους καὶ οὐχὶ τοῦ φωτός,
οἱ δὲ θυρωροὶ τῆς σκοτίας κληρονομήσουσιν αὐτοῦ
τὴν δόξαν καὶ τὴν εὐπρέπειαν.

41.7	filled Sslav: inspired (empneustheis) PV
41.7	"Paraleipomena" of Eliphaz (see 40.14 note)--possibly this is an allusion to the lament now found in 32.1-12. The possible confusion of "Eliphaz" and "Elious" in chs. 31-35 and 39-44 is a major problem for text and tradition criticism in T.Job
42.1	stopped SV: + his tirade P (see 41.1 and Job 38.1 gk)
42.1	who censured (lit. "he spoke censuring")...and showed SV: he spoke and censured...showing P
42.2	om entire verse V
42.2	they (or possibly "I") Sslav: the four kings also P
42.3a	the Lord said to Eliphaz SV: he said to (pros) Eliphaz--Why (ti ē) Eliphas (have) P
42.3b	two SP: om V
42.5	your SP: this V
42.8	made SP: offered V
43.1	the Lord SP: he V

.7	(6)	Then Elious, filled with Satan, uttered arrogant words against me, which are recorded in the "Paraleipomena" of Eliphaz.
42.1	(2)	And after he stopped, there appeared to me through a tempest and clouds the Lord, who censured Elious and showed me that the one
.2	(3)	who spoke in him was not man but beast. And when the Lord spoke to me through the cloud, they heard the voice of the one who was
.3a	(4)	speaking to me. And after the Lord stopped speaking to me, the Lord said to Eliphaz:
.3b	(5)	You and your two friends sinned.
.4		For you have not spoken truly against my servant Job.
.5	(6)	So arise and have him offer up sacrifices on your behalf
.6		so that your sin might be taken away. For if it were not for him, I would have destroyed you!
.7		And they brought me the things for sacrifice.
.8		And taking them, I made an offering on their behalf and the Lord accepted it and forgave their sin.
43.1		Then when Eliphaz, Baldas and Sophar knew that the Lord had graciously forgiven their sin but had not considered Elious
	(2)	worthy, Eliphaz in turn recited a hymn,
	(3)	while the other friends and their troops made response <to him>
.2a	(4)	near the altar. Eliphaz spoke thus:
.2b		Our sin was cancelled and our lawlessness removed;
.2c	(5)	Elious, the only wicked one, will have no memorial among the living.
.3a		And his lamp, extinguished, obliterated its light;
.3b	(6)	and the splendor of his lantern will depart from him for condemnation.
.4a		For this one is <the one> of darkness and not of light,
.4b		and the doorkeepers of darkness shall inherit his splendor and majesty.

43.1	sin SP: + because of his servant Job V
43.1	but PV: + then S
43.1	worthy SP: + of forgiveness (lit. "concession") V
43.1	Eliphaz in turn (lit. "resuming") V: pr and (de) S; Eliphas receiving (analabon) a spirit P
43.1	response <to him> PV (see 31.8, 33.1): response S [the preserved gk witnesses do not repeat a standard response here, as in ch.32 (see also 25.1-7), but cop repeats 43.2b-c = 43.13 at least after 43.4b and 43.6b (cop om 43.5 entirely)]
43.2a	Eliphaz S: pr And V; Eliphas P (see 29.3a note)
43.2b	sin SV: sins (were) P (see 43.13a)
43.2b	removed SV: buried P
43.2c	Elious S: + Elious P; but Elious Vslav
43.4a	this one is <the one> P: this one is S; he is a son V
43.4b	and majesty SPV: om cop (? in lacuna) + refrain (see 43.1 note)

.5 (7)   ἡ βασιλεία αὐτοῦ παρῆλθεν σέσηπται αὐτοῦ ὁ θρόνος,
          καὶ ἡ τιμὴ τοῦ σκήματος ⟨αὐτοῦ⟩ ἐν τῷ ᾅδῃ τυγχάνει·
.6 (8)   ἠγάπησεν τὸ τοῦ ὄφεως κάλλος καὶ τὰς λεπίδας τοῦ δράκοντος,
          ἡ δὲ χολὴ αὐτοῦ καὶ ὁ ἰὸς αὐτοῦ εἰς βορρᾶν·
.7 (9)   οὐκ ἐκτήσατο ἑαυτῷ τὸν κύριον οὐδὲ ἐφοβήθη αὐτόν,
          ἀλλὰ καὶ τοὺς ἐντίμους αὐτοῦ παρώργισεν·
.8 (10)   ἐπελάθετο αὐτοῦ ὁ κύριος καὶ οἱ ἅγιοι ἐγκατέλιπον αὐτόν,
   (11)   ἡ δὲ ὀργὴ καὶ ὁ θυμὸς ἔσται αὐτῷ εἰς κένωμα·
.9   οὐκ ἔχει ἔλεος ἐν καρδίᾳ αὐτοῦ οὐδὲ εἰρήνην
          ⟨ἐν στόματι αὐτοῦ⟩
   (12)   ἰὸν ἀσπίδος ἔσχεν ἐν τῇ γλώσσῃ αὐτοῦ·
.10(13)   δίκαιός ἐστιν ὁ κύριος, ἀληθινὰ αὐτοῦ τὰ κρίματα,
          παρ' ᾧ οὐκ ἔστιν προσωποληψία, κρινεῖ γὰρ ἡμᾶς ὁμοθυμαδόν.
.11(14)   ἰδοὺ ὁ κύριος παρεγένετο, ἰδοὺ οἱ ἅγιοι ἡτοιμάσθησαν,
          προηγουμένων τῶν στεφάνων τῶν ἐγκωμίων·
.12(15)   χαιρέτωσαν οἱ ἅγιοι, ἀγαλλιάσθωσαν αἱ καρδίαι αὐτῶν
   (16)   ὅτι ἀπείληφαν τὴν δόξαν ἣν προσεδόκησαν·
.13(17)   ἦρται τὰ ἁμαρτήματα ἡμῶν, κεκαθάρισται ἡμῶν ἡ ἀνομία,
          ὁ δὲ πονηρὸς Ἐλιοῦς ἐν τοῖς ζῶσιν μνημόσυνον οὐκ ἔσχεν·

44.1   Μετὰ δὲ τὸ παύσασθαι Ἐλιφὰζ τοῦ ὕμνου ἐπιφωνούντων αὐτῷ
          πάντων καὶ κυκλούντων ἀναστάντες εἰσήλθομεν εἰς τὴν πόλιν
   (2)   εἰς ἣν οἰκοῦμεν οἰκίαν καὶ πεποιήκαμεν εὐωχίας ἐν τῇ
.2   τερπνότητι τοῦ κυρίου. καὶ πάλιν ἐπεζήτησα εὐεργεσίας
.3   ποιεῖν τοῖς πτωχοῖς. καὶ παρεγένοντο πρός με ⟨πάντες⟩ οἱ
.4   φίλοι μου καὶ ὅσοι ᾔδεισαν με εὐποιοῦντα· καὶ ἠρώτησαν με
          λέγοντες
          τί παρ' ἡμῶν ⟨νῦν⟩ αἰτεῖς;
.5   ἐγὼ δὲ ἀναμνησθεὶς τῶν πτωχῶν τοῦ πάλιν εὐποιεῖν ᾐτησάμην
          λέγων
          δότε μοι ἕκαστος ἀμνάδα ⟨μίαν εἰς ἔνδυσιν τῶν πτωχῶν
          τῶν ἐν γυμνώσει ὄντων.

43.5   om entire verse cop (see 43.1 note)
43.5b   honor (or "value," "price") of ⟨his⟩ (om S) pretence (lit.
        "appearance") SV: honor of his tent (skēnōmatos) P
43.6a   the scales SPV: om cop
43.6b   food SPV: + refrain cop (see 43.1 note)
43.8b   emptiness SV: a tent (skēnōma) P
43.9a   ⟨in his mouth⟩ cj James: in his body (sōmati) P: om SVslav
43.9b   an asp SVslav: asps P
43.10b for SV: om P
43.10b us PV: you S
43.11b of eulogies (or "laudatory odes") S: and the eulogies V; with eulogies P
43.12a their hearts exult SVslav: them exult in heart P
43.13a sins S(V): sin P (see 43.2b !); + and V

.5a (7)   His kingdom has passed away, his throne has decayed,
.5b   and the honor of <his> pretense is in hades.
.6a (8)   He loved the beauty of the serpent and the scales of the dragon,
.6b   and its venom and poison are his for food.
.7a (9)   He did not acquire the Lord for his own, nor did he fear him,
.7b   but even his honored ones he provoked to anger.
.8a (10)   The Lord has forgotten him and the holy ones have forsaken him,
.8b (11)   but wrath and anger will be his for emptiness.
.9a   He has no hope in his heart, nor peace <in his mouth>,
.9b (12)   he had the poison of an asp in his tongue.
.10a(13)   Righteous is the Lord, trustworthy are his judgments,
.10b   with him there is no favoritism, for he will judge us consistently.
.11a(14)   Behold, the Lord has drawn near, behold his holy ones
                have been prepared,
.11b   while the crowns of encomia lead the way.
.12a(15)   Let the holy ones rejoice, let their hearts exult,
.12b(16)   for they have received the splendor which they awaited.
.13a(17)   Gone are our sins, cleansed is our lawlessness,
.13b   and the evil Elious has no memorial among the living.

44.1   And after Eliphaz stopped the hymn, while they were all making
            response to him and circling about, we arose and entered the city
      (2)   in which we have a house and we held festivities in the delight
.2   of the Lord. And again I sought to do good works for the poor.
.3   And <all> my friends and as many as knew me as a benefactor
.4a   came to me. And they questioned me saying,
.4b   What are you asking from us <now>?
.5a   And remembering to do good to the poor again, I made a request
            saying,
.5b   Let each of you give me one <lamb for clothing the poor who
                are naked.

44.1   while - about (+ the altar P) S(P): om V
44.1   all...to him P (see 31.8, 43.1): all of them (autōn) S
44.1   in which we SV: + now P
44.1   we held (+ great P) festivities S(P): they held a feast for me V
44.2   om entire verse V
44.2   And S: om P
44.3   <all> PV: om S
44.3   me as a benefactor SV: to do good (eupoiein) P
44.4a   And SP: om V
44.4b   <now> PV: om S
44.5a   remembering SP: undertaking V
44.5b-6 <lamb - one> PV: om S (haplography)

.6 (5) καὶ τότε ἕκαστος προσήνεγκέν μοι ἀμνάδα> μίαν καὶ
.7 τετράδραχμον χρυσίου· καὶ τότε ὁ κύριος εὐλόγησεν πάντα
ὅσα <μοι> ὑπῆρχεν καὶ πεποίηκέν μοι ἐν τῷ διπλῷ.

45.1 Καὶ νῦν, τέκνα μου, ἰδοὺ ἐγὼ τελευτῶ·
.2 μόνον μὴ ἐπιλάθεσθε τοῦ κυρίου·
.3 (2) εὐποιήσατε τοῖς πτωχοῖς, μὴ παρίδητε τοὺς ἀδυνάτους·
.4 (3) μὴ λάβετε ἑαυτοῖς γυναῖκας ἐκ τῶν ἀλλοτρίων.
.5 (4) ἰδοὺ οὖν, τέκνα μου, διαμεριῶ ὑμῖν πάντα ὅσα μοι ὑπάρχει
πρὸς τὸ δεσπόζειν ἕκαστος καὶ ἔχειν ἐξουσίαν ἀγαθοποιῆσαι
ἕκαστος ἐκ τοῦ μέρους αὐτοῦ ἀκωλύτως.

46.1 Οἱ δὲ παρήνεγκαν τὰ ὄντα εἰς μερισμὸν αὐτοῖς τοῖς ἑπτὰ ἄρρεσιν·
.2 καὶ ἀπὸ τῶν χρημάτων οὐ παρέσχεν ταῖς θηλείαις·
.3 αἱ δὲ λυπηθεῖσαι εἶπον τῷ πατρί
κύριε πάτερ ἡμῶν, μὴ καὶ ἡμεῖς <οὐκ> ἐσμὲν τέκνα σου;
διότι οὐκ ἔδωκας ἡμῖν ἐκ τῶν ὄντων σοι;
.4 (3) εἶπεν δὲ Ἰὼβ ταῖς θηλείαις
μὴ ταραχθῆτε, θυγατέρες μου, οὐ γὰρ ὑμῶν ἐπελαθόμην·
.5 (4) ἤδη γὰρ ὑμῖν ἔπεμψα κληρονομίαν κρείττονα τῆς τῶν ἑπτὰ
ἀδελφῶν ὑμῶν.
.6 (5) καὶ τότε καλέσας τὴν θυγατέραν αὐτοῦ τὴν λεγομένην Ἡμέραν
λέγει αὐτῇ
λαβοῦσα τὸ δακτύλιον ὕπαγε εἰς τὴν κέλλαν καὶ ἔνεγκέ μοι
τὰ τρία σκρίνια τοῦ χρυσίου ἵνα δώσω ὑμῖν τὴν κληρονομίαν.
.7 (6) ἡ δὲ ἀπελθοῦσα ἤνεγκεν αὐτά·
.8 (7) καὶ ἤνοιξεν καὶ ἐξήνεγκεν τὰς <τρεῖς χορδὰς τὰς> ποικίλας ὡς
(8) μὴ δύνασθαί τινα ἄνθρωπον λαλῆσαι περὶ τῆς εἰδέας αὐτῶν ἐπεὶ

44.6 gold SP: + and silver V
44.6 tetradrachm PV [usually designates a silver coin worth about 50 cents, or about 1/4 oz of weight]: tetragram S [weighing about 1/6 oz (4 scruples), used with reference to gold coins]
44.7 then SV: om P
44.7 and doubled them for me S(P): and within a few days I abounded with goods and cattle and the rest of what I had lost, and I received others double, and I also took your mother as wife and fathered you ten in place of my ten children that had died V
45.1 my children SP: + I command you V
45.1 dying SP: + You than, must take my place V
45.5 and each (om V) - share SV: of his own share unhindered P
46.1 notice the return to third person narrative (=1.1-2a)
46.1 And - males SP: And having said this, he brought forth all his goods and distributed them among his seven male sons V
46.2 And SV: For P
46.3a And they were distressed SP: om V
46.3b <not>PV: om S
46.3b a portion of SP: an\inheritance from V

.6	(5)	And then each one brought me one> lamb and one gold tetradrachm
.7		coin. And then the Lord blessed all my possessions and doubled them for me.
45.1		And now, my children, behold I am dying.
.2		Above all, do not forget the Lord.
.3	(2)	Do good to the poor, do not overlook the helpless.
.4	(3)	Do not take wives for yourselves from foreigners.
.5	(4)	Behold then, my children, I shall divide all my possessions among you, so each of you has legal control and each has the resources to do good works unhindered from his share.
46.1		And they brought forth the property for distribution to the seven
.2		males. And he did not present any of the goods to the females.
.3a		And they were distressed and said to their father:
.3b		Our father, sir, it can't be that we are <not> also your children, can it? Why did you not give us a portion of your property?
.4a	(3)	But Job said to the females:
.4b		Do not be upset, my daughters, for I did not forget you.
.5	(4)	For I have already selected for you an inheritance better than that of your seven brothers.
.6a	(5)	And then when he had called his daughter named Hemera, he said to her:
.6b		Take the signet ring, go to the chamber and bring me the three golden boxes so that I may give you the inheritance.
.7	(6)	And she went away and brought them.
.8	(7)	And he opened them and brought forth <three bands>, shimmering, so
	(8)	that no man could describe their form, since they are not

---

46.4a	the females SP: his daughters V
46.5	For...already S: For behold (<u>idou</u>) V; Already P
46.5	selected (lit. "sent") SP: saved (<u>sphylaxa</u>) V
46.5	of your SP: which your...received V
46.6a	And then S: And V; then P
46.6b	Take the signet ring: or perhaps "Take (hold of) the door handle/ring"
46.6b	chamber S: vault (<u>krypten</u>) P; treasury/store-room (<u>tameion</u>) V; room slav
46.6b	me SVslav: om P
46.6b	three SP: om V
46.6b	boxes S: implements/vessels (skeu<a>ria) P; vessel (? <u>skeneion</u> ?) V
46.6b	the inheritance SP: your inheritance V
46.7,8	them SP: it V
46.8	And PV: + then S
46.8	<three bands>(or perhaps better, "corded objects"), shimmering P: three girdle bands V; the shimmering (items) S [it is not clear what is being pictured here--<u>chordē</u> often designates a gut band or string (as for musical instruments), while <u>poikilē</u> can indicate complexity of various sorts (multicolored, spotted, changeable, intricate, etc.); perhaps a network of cords (knotted?) is envisioned, or phylactery-like objects with long cords (see 47.11)]

.9 μὴ εἶναι ἐκ τῆς γῆς, ἀλλὰ τοῦ οὐρανοῦ εἰσιν, ἐξαστράπτουσαι
σπινθῆραις φωτίναις ὡς ἀκτῖνες τοῦ ἡλίου. καὶ δέδωκεν χορδὴν
μίαν ἑκάστης τῶν θυγατέρων εἰπών

λάβετε αὐτὰς περὶ τὸ στῆθος ὑμῶν ἵνα εὖ ὑμῖν γένηται
πάσας τὰς ἡμέρας τῆς ζωῆς ὑμῶν.

47.1 εἶπεν δὲ αὐτῷ ἡ ἄλλη θυγατὴρ ἡ λεγομένη Κασσία
πάτερ, αὕτη ἐστὶν ἡ κληρονομία ἣν ἔλεγες εἶναι κρείττονα
.2 τῆς τῶν ἀδελφῶν ἡμῶν; τί οὖν τὸ περιττὸν τούτων τῶν χορδῶν--
μὴ ἐκ τούτων ἕξομεν τοῦ ζῆν;
.3 (2) καὶ εἶπεν αὐταῖς ὁ πατήρ
 (3) οὐ μόνον ἐκ τούτων τὸ ζῆν ἕξετε, ἀλλὰ καὶ αὗται αἱ χορδαὶ
εἰσάξουσιν ὑμᾶς εἰς τὸν μείζονα αἰῶνα <ζῆσαι> ἐν τοῖς
.4 οὐρανοῖς. ἀγνοεῖτε οὖν, τέκνα μου, τὴν τιμὴν τῶν σπάρτων
τούτων ὧν με κατηξίωσεν ὁ κύριος ἐν ἡμέρᾳ ᾗ ἠβουλήθη
ἐλεῆσαι με καὶ περιαρθῆναι ἐκ τοῦ σώματός μου τὰς πληγὰς
.5 καὶ τοὺς σκώληκας· καλέσας με παρέθετο μοι ταύτας τὰς τρεῖς
χορδὰς λέγων μοι

ἀνάστας ζῶσαι ὥσπερ ἀνὴρ τὴν ὀσφῦν σου·
.6 ἐρωτήσω δέ σε, σὺ δέ μοι ἀποκρίθητι.
.7 (6) ἐγὼ δὲ λαβὼν περιεξωσάμην, καὶ εὐθέως ἀφανεῖς ἐγένοντο
οἱ σκώληκες ἀπὸ τοῦ σώματός μου, <ὁμοίως δὲ καὶ αἱ πληγαί·>
.8 (7) καὶ λοιπὸν τὸ σῶμά μου ἐνίσχυεν διὰ κυρίου ὡς ὅτι οὐδὲ
.9 (8) ὅλως πεπόνθα τι· ἀλλὰ καὶ τῶν ἐν τῇ καρδίᾳ μου ὀδυνῶν λήθην
.10(9) ἔσχον· ὁ δὲ κύριος λελάληκέν μοι ἐν δυνάμει ὑποδείξας μοι
.11(10) τὰ γενόμενα καὶ τὰ μέλλοντα. νῦν οὖν, τέκνα μου, ἔχουσαι
αὐτὰς οὐχ ἕξετε ὅλως ἀντιτασσόμενον τὸν ἐχθρόν, ἀλλ' οὐδὲ
 (11) τὰς ἐνθυμήσεις αὐτοῦ ἐν τῇ διανοίᾳ ὑμῶν, διότι φυλακτήριον
.12 ἐστιν τοῦ κυρίου. ἐξεγερθεῖσαι οὖν περιζώσασθε <αὐ>τὰς
πρὶν τελευτήσω, ἵνα δυνηθῆτε θεάσασθαι τοὺς ἐρχομένους εἰς
τὴν ἐμὴν ἔξοδον ὅπως θαυμάσητε τὰ τοῦ θεοῦ κτίσματα.

46.9a   each - one S: each one...one V; one P [see p.8]
46.9b   Place - life SP: Take these and be girded so that they may
        protect you throughout the days of your life and supply
        every good thing V
46.9b   well S: om P
47.1b   brothers PV: other (allōn) brothers S
47.2   What SV: Who P
47.2   is so - bands S: has a use for these unusual bands P; om V
47.3b   bands SP: om V
47.3b   also SV: om P
47.3b   <to live> PV: om S
47.4   Are you ignorant then SP: Or are you ignorant V
47.4   my children SV: children P
47.4   cords SP: items (parontōn) V
47.4   on which he wished/desired SP: the Lord was pleased (eudokēsen) V

		from earth but are from heaven, flashing with bright sparks like rays
.9a		of the sun. And he gave each of the daughters one band saying,
.9b		Place these around your breast so that it may go well with you all the days of your life.
47.1		And the other daughter, named Kassia, said to him:
.1b		Father, is this the inheritance which you said was better than
.2		that of our brothers? What then is so unusual about these bands? We won't be able to sustain our life from them, will we?
.3a	(2)	And the father said to them,
.3b	(3)	Not only will you sustain life from these, but these bands will also lead you into the better world, <to live> in the heavens.
.4		Are you ignorant, then, my children, of the value of these cords, of which the Lord considered me worthy on the day on which he wished to have mercy on me and remove from my body the diseases
.5a		and the worms? When he called me he set before me these three bands and said to me:
.5b		Arise, gird your loins like a man!
.6		I shall question you, and you answer me.
.7	(6)	So I took them and girded myself, and immediately the worms disappeared from my body <and the plagues as well>.
.8	(7)	And then, through the Lord, my body grew strong as if it
.9	(8)	had not suffered anything at all. But I could even forget
.10	(9)	the pains in my heart! And the Lord spoke to me by a powerful act, showing me things present and things to come.
.11	(10)	Now then, my children, since you have them you will not have the enemy opposing you at all, neither will you have anxieties
	(11)	about him in your mind, because it is a protective amulet of the
.12		Lord. Rise, then, gird them around you before I die in order that you may be able to see those who are coming for my departure, so that you may marvel at the creatures of God.

47.4	remove SV: cure (perigraphēnai) P
47.5a	When SP: pr For V
47.7	disappeared SV: + from that time onward (apo tote) P
47.7	<and - well> PV: om S
47.8	strong SP: + and thus I went on V
47.10	by a powerful act (lit. "in power") or "through a powerful agent"
47.11	them SV: these (tautas) P
47.11	the enemy opposing you PV: to oppose the enemy S
47.11	anxieties about him (ot "his ideas") SP: anxieties V
47.11	protective amulet: or "phylactery," perhaps simply "safeguard"
47.11	Lord SVslav: Father P (see 33.3,9; 40.3; [50.3]; 52.6)
47.12	them P: yourselves (heautas)V; tas S
47.12	those SP: + angels V
47.12	departure (or "exodus") SV: soul P
47.12	creatures SP: powers (or "mighty acts/ones" --see 47.10) V

TESTAMENT OF JOB

48.1 οὕτως ἀναστᾶσα ἡ μία τῶν τριῶν θυγατέρων ⟨ἡ καλουμένη⟩ Ἡμέρα
.2 περιείληξεν ἑαυτὴν καθὼς εἶπεν ὁ πατήρ· καὶ ἀνέλαβεν ἄλλην
.3 καρδίαν ὡς μηκέτι φρονεῖν τὰ τῆς γῆς· ἀπεφθέγξατο δὲ τῇ
ἀγγελικῇ φωνῇ καὶ ὕμνον ἀνέπεμπεν τῷ θεῷ κατὰ τὴν τῶν ἀγγέλων
.4 ὑμνολογίαν· καὶ ὡς ἀπεφθέξατο τοὺς ὕμνους, εἴασεν τὸ πνεῦμα
ἐν στολῇ τῇ ἑαυτῆς κεχαραγμένον.

49.1 Καὶ τότε ἡ Κασσία περιεζώσατο καὶ ἔσχεν τὴν καρδίαν
.2 ἀλλοιωθεῖσαν ὡς μηκέτι ἐνθυμηθῆναι τὰ κοσμικά· καὶ τὸ μὲν
στόμα αὐτῆς ἔλαβεν τὴν διάλεκτον τῶν ἀρχόντων, ⟨ἐδοξολόγησεν
.3 δὲ τοῦ ὑψηλοῦ τόπου τὸ ποίημα.⟩ διότι εἴ τις βούλεται γνῶναι
τὸ ποίημα τῶν οὐρανῶν, δυνήσεται εὑρεῖν ἐν τοῖς ὕμνοις Κασσίας.

50.1 Καὶ τότε περιεζώσατο καὶ ἡ ἄλλη ἡ καλουμένη Ἀμαλθείας-κέρας
(2) καὶ ἔσχεν στόμα ἀποφθεγγόμενον ἐν τῇ διαλέκτῳ τῶν ἐν ὕψει, ἐπεὶ
καὶ αὐτῆς ἡ καρδία ἠλλοιοῦτο ἀφισταμένη ἀπὸ τῶν κοσμικῶν·
.2 λελάληκεν δὲ ἐν τῇ διαλέκτῳ ⟨τῶν⟩ Χερουβὶμ δοξολογοῦσα τὸν
.3 δεσπότην τῶν ἀρετῶν ἐνδειξαμένη τὴν δόξαν αὐτῶν· καὶ ὁ
βουλόμενος λοιπὸν ⟨ἴχνος καταλαβεῖν τῆς πατρικῆς δόξης⟩
εὑρήσει ἀναγεγραμμένον ἐν ταῖς εὐχαῖς τῆς Ἀμαλθείας-κέρας.

51.1 (1-2) Μετὰ δὲ τὸ παύσασθαι τὰς τρεῖς ὑμνολογούσας, ἐπικειμένου τοῦ
κυρίου καὶ ἐμοῦ Νηρεὸς ἀδελφοῦ ὄντος τοῦ Ἰώβ, ἐπικειμένου
(3) τοῦ ἁγίου ἀγγέλου, ἐκαθεζόμην πλησίον τοῦ Ἰὼβ ἐπὶ τῆς κλίνης·
.2 καὶ ἤκουσα κἀγὼ τὰ μεγαλεῖα μιᾶς ὑποσημειουμένης τῇ μιᾷ·
.3 (4) καὶ ἀνεγραψάμην τὸ βιβλίον ⟨σημείων πλείστων τῶν ὕμνων παρὰ
τῶν τριῶν θυγατέρων τοῦ ἀδελφοῦ μου⟩ σωτήριον εἶναι ταῦτα
μετὰ τούτων, ὅτι ταῦτά ἐστιν τὰ μεγαλεῖα τοῦ θεοῦ.

48.1	Thus SP: Now V
48.1	of the three daughters ⟨called⟩ cj Kraft: of them called V; of the three daughters S; called P
48.1	wrapped SP: girded V (as 49.1, 50.1)
48.1	herself S (slav): her cord around (<u>sparten</u>; see 47.4) P; + and immediately left her own flesh V
48.1	her (lit. "the") SP: her V
48.3	chanted verses SP: chanted angelic hymns V
48.3	language (lit. "voice") SV: dialect P (as in 49.2, 50.2, 52.4)
48.3	ascribed SP: raised the strain of V
48.4	om entire verse V [judging from the parallels in 49.3 and 50.3, we might expect reference to a specific poem and a collection identified with Hemera; thus "the Spirit" (cj Kraft "the poem" =49.3) is taken to be a title. Schwartz emends <u>stole</u> to "epistle" (so Spittler) with similar results.]
48.4	as she - she permitted "the Spirit" (or "the Spirit permitted [it]") S: the spirit permitted the hymns she chanted P
49.1	then SP: + the other daughter also V (see 50.1)
49.1	anxious about (or "desired") --see 47.11
49.2	archons, heavenly rulers/powers
49.2	⟨and - place⟩ PV: om S [this could also be rendered "glorified God with the poem of the ex.pl.," or "glorified the creature (see 47.12) of the ex.pl."]

48.1 Thus, when the one of the three daughters <called> Hemera arose, she wrapped herself just as her father said.
.2 And she received another heart, so that she no longer thought
.3 about earthly things. And she chanted verses in the angelic language, and acribed a hymn to God in accord with the hymnic
.4 style of the angels. And as she chanted the hymns, she permitted "the Spirit" to be inscribed on her garment.

49.1 And then Kassia girded herself and had her heart changed so that
.2 she was no longer anxious about worldly things. And her mouth received the dialect of the archons, <and glorified the creation of
.3 the exalted place>. Wherefore if anyone wishes to know "the creation of the heavens," he will be able to find it in the "Hymns of Kassia."

50.1 And then the other one also, called Amaltheias-keras, girded herself and her mouth chanted verses in the dialect of those on
(2) high, since her heart also was changed by withdrawing from
.2 worldly things. And she spoke in the dialect of <the> cherubim, glorifying the master of virtues by exhibiting their splendor.
.3 And the one who further wishes <to grasp the poetic rhythm of "the paternal splendor"> will find it recorded in the "Prayers of Amaltheias-keras."

51.1 (1-2)And after the three had stopped singing hymns, while the Lord was present as was I Nereos the brother of Job, while the holy
.2 (3) angel was present, I was sitting near Job on the couch. And even I heard the magnificent compositions, as each [sister] noted
.3 (4) things down for the other. And I wrote out the book <of notations for most of the hymns that issued from the three daughters of my brother,> so that these things would serve as a safeguard along with those, for these are the magnificent compositions of God.

50.1   And SP: om V
50.2   And SV: For P
50.3   < to - "splendor"> (P)V: om S ["poetic rhythm" (lit. "footstep," "trace"); P adds "of Hemera" (or "of day"), perhaps reflecting the problem at 48.4 (see above)]
51.1   while - I was S(P): I Nereos, the brother of Job was Vslav
51.1   angel S: spirit P
51.1   on the (my P, his slav) couch (or "bed") SP: while he reclined V
51.2   And even S: and V; om P
51.2   compositions SP: + of the 3 daughters of my brother V
51.2   noted things down for (? or "made signs to"?) SP: spun around (? hyposiōmenēs) V
51.3   book - <brother> cj Kraft (see P): entire (holon) book...(etc.) P; this book in addition to (or "except for") the hymns and the notations of the word/line/verse (rhēmatos) V ; book S
51.3   safeguard (lit. "saving"; see 47.11): or perhaps "thank-offering"
51.3   with those S: om PV

52.1   Καὶ μετὰ τρεῖς ἡμέρας ποιουμένου τοῦ Ἰὼβ νοσεῖν ἐπὶ τῆς
          κλίνης ἄνευ πόνου καὶ ὀδυνῶν ἐπεὶ μὴ ἴσχυεν πόνος ἅπτεσθαι
   (2)   αὐτοῦ διὰ τὸ σημεῖον τῆς περιζώσεως ἧς περιεζώσατο--καὶ μετὰ
          τρεῖς ἡμέρας εἶδεν τοὺς ἐλθόντας ἐπὶ τὴν ψυχὴν αὐτοῦ·
 .2 (3)   καὶ εὐθέως ἀναστὰς ἔλαβεν κιθάραν καὶ ἔδωκεν τῇ θυγατρὶ αὐτοῦ
    (4)   Ἡμέρα, τῇ δὲ Κασσία ἔδωκεν θυμιατήριον, τῇ δὲ Ἀμαλθείας-κέρας
    (5)   ἔδωκεν τύμπανον--ὅπως εὐλογήσωσιν τοὺς ἐλθόντας ἐπὶ τὴν ψυχὴν
 .3 (6-7) αὐτοῦ· αἱ δὲ λαβοῦσαι καὶ ηὐλόγησαν ⟨καὶ ἐδοξολόγησαν⟩ τὸν
 .4 (8)   θεὸν ἐν τῇ ἐξαιρέτῳ διαλέκτῳ. ⟨καὶ⟩ μετὰ ταῦτα ἐξῆλθεν
          ὁ ἐπικαθήμενος τῷ μεγάλῳ ἅρματι καὶ ἠσπάσατο τὸν Ἰώβ,
    (9)   βλεπουσῶν τῶν τριῶν θυγατέρων καὶ αὐτοῦ τοῦ πατρὸς αὐτῶν
 .5 (10) βλέποντος, ἄλλων δὲ μὴ βλεπόντων· λαβὼν δὲ τὴν ψυχὴν ἀνεπετάσθη
          ἐπαγκαλιζόμενος αὐτὴν καὶ ἀνεβίβασεν αὐτὴν ἐπὶ τὸ ἅρμα καὶ
 .6 (11) ὥδευσεν ἐπὶ ἀνατολάς· τὸ δὲ σῶμα αὐτοῦ περισταλὲν ἀπηνέχθη
    (12) εἰς τὸν τάφον προηγουμένων τῶν τριῶν θυγατέρων αὐτοῦ καὶ
          περιεζωσμένων καὶ ὑμνολογουσῶν ἐν ὕμνοις τὸν θεόν.

53.1   Κἀγὼ τότε Νηρεὸς ὁ ἀδελφὸς ⟨αὐτοῦ⟩ μετὰ τῶν τέκνων τῶν
          ἀρρεν⟨ικῶν⟩ σὺν τοῖς πένησιν καὶ ὀρφανοῖς καὶ πᾶσιν τοῖς
    (2)   ἀδυνάτοις κλαιόντων καὶ λεγόντων
          οὐαὶ ἡμῖν σήμερον ⟨ὅτι σήμερον⟩ ἦρται ἡ δύναμις τῶν ἀδυνάτων,
 .2 (3)   τὸ φῶς τῶν τυφλῶν, ὁ πατὴρ τῶν ὀρφανῶν· ἦρται ὁ ⟨τῶν⟩ ξένων
 .3   ξενοδόχος, τῶν ἀδυνάτων ἡ ὁδός· ἦρται τῶν γυμνῶν ἡ ἔνδυσις,
 .4   τῶν χηρῶν ὁ ὑπερασπιστής. τίς λοιπὸν οὐ κλαύσει τὸν ἄνθρωπον
          τοῦ θεοῦ;

52.1a   And - presumed to be SP: Therefore, while Job was lying V
52.1a   pains SV: pain P
52.1a   touch him S: + any longer (eti) PV
52.1a   omen (lit. "sign" or "mark")--possibly referring to the power of
           the "sash" itself, or to some "notation" it may have
           contained (see 47.11, 51.3)
52.1b   he saw SP: Job saw V
52.1b   those SP: + holy angels V
52.2   those SP: + holy angels V
52.3   taken them S: + they saw the flashing chariots coming for his soul P;
           + they were chanting/singing and playing (the instruments) V
52.3   ⟨and glorified⟩ (P)V: om S
52.3   God SV: each P
52.4   ⟨And⟩ PV: om S
52.4   (he) greeted SP: they greeted V
52.4   the...daughters SP: his...daughters also V
52.4   and their (the P) - looked on SP: om V
52.4   others SV: certain others P
52.5   taking the soul SP: he took the soul of Job and V

52.1a   And after three days, while Job was presumed to be sick on the couch,
        without suffering or pains since suffering could not touch him
   .1b (2) because of the omen of the sash with which he was girded--and after
   .2 (3) three days he saw those who had come for his soul. And rising
        immediately, he took a lyre and gave it to his daughter Hemera,
       (4) and gave a censer to Kassia, and gave a kettle-drum to
       (5) Amaltheias-keras--so that they might praise those who had come
   .3 (6) for his soul. And when they had taken them,
       (7) they praised <and glorified> God in the exalted dialect.
   .4 (8) <And> after these things, the one who sat in the great chariot came
       (9) out and greeted Job, while the three daughters looked on, and their
   .5 (10) father himself looked on, but others did not see. And taking the
        soul, he flew up while embracing it, and made it mount the chariot,
   .6 (11) and set off for the east. But his body, wrapped for burial, was
      (12) borne to the tomb as his three daughters led the way, girded about
        and singing hymns to God.

53.1a   And then I Nereos, <his> brother, with the male children,
        accompanied by the poor and the orphans and all the helpless--
       (2) we were weeping and saying:
   .1b   Woe to us today, <for today> there has been taken away the strength
       (3) of the helpless, the light of the blind, the father of the orphans.
   .2   Taken away is the host of <the> strangers, the path of the weak.
   .3   Taken away is the clothing of the naked, the protector of the
   .4   widows. Who then will not weep for the man of God?

52.5   made it mount SV: mounted P
52.6   wrapped (or "laid out," "covered") for burial SP: om V
52.6   girded about SP: + with bands V
52.6   and singing SV: singing P
52.6   God SVslav: the Father P (see 47.11 note)
53.1a   then SV: om P [on the syntax of this passage, see p.8]
53.1a   <his> PV: om S
53.1a   with the(+seven P)-children S(P)slav: and his seven sons (paides) V
53.1a   the poor...and all SP: the rest of the people and poor
            (ptōchois)...(om) V
53.1a   weeping and S(P): they mourned with great mourning over him V
53.1b   today, <for today> cj Kraft: today Sslav; for today V;
            today, double woe, for today P
53.1b   away SP: + from us V
53.1b   the light...the father SV: taken away is the light...taken away is
            the father P
53.2   of <the> (om S) strangers SP: om V
53.2   the path of the weak (of those who go astray V) S(V)slav: om P
53.3   Taken away SP: om V
53.3   clothing SP: covering (skepasma) V
53.3   of the naked, the protector SVslav: om P

.5 καὶ ἅμα περιεκύκλωσαν αὐτὸν πᾶσαι αἱ χῆραι καὶ οἱ ὀρφανοὶ
.6 (6-7) κωλύοντες αὐτῷ μὴ εἰσεναχθῆναι εἰς τὸν τάφον· καὶ μετὰ τρεῖς
ἡμέρας ἀπέθεντο αὐτὸν ἐν τῷ τάφῳ ὡς ἐν καλῷ ὕπνῳ, λαβόντα
ὄνομα ὀνομαστὸν ἐν πάσαις ⟨ταῖς⟩ γενε⟨αῖ⟩ς τοῦ αἰῶνος.

subscript of S

Ἔζησεν δὲ Ἰὼβ μετὰ τὴν πληγὴν ἔτη $\overline{\rho o}$·
ὁ δὲ ὅλος χρόνος τῆς ζωῆς αὐτοῦ $\overline{\sigma \mu \eta}$·
καὶ εἶδεν τοὺς υἱοὺς τῶν υἱῶν αὐτοῦ ⟨εἰς⟩ τετάρτην γενεάν.

subscript of V

Καταλείψας υἱοὺς $\overline{\zeta}$ καὶ θυγατέρας τρεῖς; καὶ οὐχ εὑρέθησαν
κατὰ τὰς θυγατέρας Ἰὼβ βελτίους αὐτῶν ἐν τοῖς ὑπ' οὐ(ρα)νὸν.
προυπῆρχε ὄνομα τῷ Ἰὼβ Ἰωβάβ, μετονομάσθη δὲ παρὰ κ(υρίο)υ Ἰώβ.
ἔζησε δὲ πρὶν τῆς πληγῆς ἔτη $\overline{\pi \varepsilon}$, μετὰ δὲ τὴν πληγὴν λαβὼν πάντα
διπλὰ ἔλαβε καὶ τὰ ἔτη διπλά, τουτέστιν $\overline{\rho o}$. τὰ δὲ πάντα ἔτη
τῆς ζωῆς αὐτοῦ $\overline{\sigma \mu \eta}$. καὶ εἶδεν υἱοὺς τῶν υἱῶν αὐτοῦ ἕως
τετάρτης γενεᾶς. γέγραπται δὲ ἀναστῆναι αὐτὸν μεθ' ὧν
ὁ κ(ύριο)ς ἀνέστησε, τῷ δὲ θ(ε)ῷ εἴη δόξα.

.5   And at once all the widows and orphans circled about him,
   (6) preventing him from being brought into the tomb.
.6 (7) And after three days they laid him in the tomb as if in a beautiful
        sleep, since he had received a name renowned in all generations
        forever.

53.5   And - tomb S: And just as they brought the body to the tomb
           all the widows...(etc. as in S) P; As they mourned deeply
           with these and similar (words), they prevented him from being
           placed in the tomb V
53.6   And SP: Thus V
53.6   as if SV: om P
53.6   name SP: good name V
53.6   forever SV: + amen Pslav

---

subscript
of S(slav)
        And Job lived after his disease 170 years.
        And the entire span of his life was 248 years.
        And he saw his sons' sons, <to> the fourth generation.

---

        disease (or "plague") S(V): + and sufferings slav
        sons' sons SV: + and great-grandsons slav
        fourth SV: third slav
        generation S: slav adds some general exhortations before closing
           with the words "glory to our God forever, amen" (see V) [for a
           translation of this material, see Spittler]

---

subscript
of V
        He left 7 sons and three daughters, and there were not found
        among those under heaven any more beautiful than Job's daughters.
        Jobab was Job's former name, but was changed by the Lord to Job.
        And he lived 85 years prior to the disease, and after the disease,
        when he received all things doubly, he also received double in
        years, that is, 170. And the total number of years of his life
        were 248, and he saw sons of his sons to the fourth generation.
        And it is written that he arose with those whom the Lord raised.
        Glory be to God!